Commentaries
on the Rite
of Christian
Initiation
of Adults

Other books in the ♆Font and Table Series

Commentaries
on the Rite
of Christian
Initiation
of Adults

Edited by
James A. Wilde

Liturgy Training Publications

The *Font and Table Series* offers pastoral perspectives on Christian baptism, confirmation and eucharistic.

General Editor: James A.Wilde

Editorial Consultants: Allan Bouley, OSB
                          professor of pastoral liturgy
                          St. John's University
                          Collegeville MN

                          Frank T. Griswold, bishop
                          Episcopal Diocese of Chicago
                          Chicago IL

                          Elizabeth Jeep
                          author, consultant
                          doctoral candidate
                          River Forest IL

                          Gordon Lathrop
                          professor of liturgy
                          Lutheran Theological Seminary
                          Philadelphia PA

                          Ron Lewinski, director
                          Office for Divine Worship
                          Catholic Archdiocese of Chicago
                          Chicago IL

Acknowledgements

Excerpts from *Rite of Christian Initiation of Adults*, copyright © 1985, International Committee on English in the Liturgy, Inc. Washington, DC. All rights reserved.

Excerpts from "National Statutes for the Catechumenate" copyright © 1988, United States Catholic Conference Washington DC. All rights reserved.

Copyright © 1988, Archdiocese of Chicago.
All rights reserved.
Liturgy Training Publications
1800 North Hermitage Avenue
Chicago IL 60622-1101
Order Phone: 312/486-7008
Editoral Phone: 312/486-8970

Printed in the United States
ISBN 0-930467-86-8

Contents

Introduction

The Father's voice calls us above the waters,
the glory of the Son shines on us,
the love of the Spirit fills us with life.

The History of the Text

By promulgating the *Constitution on the Sacred Liturgy* on December 4, 1963, the Second Vatican Council prescribed the revision of the rite of baptism of adults and decreed that the catechumenate for adults be restored in several stages. This was to be done so that the catechumenate, a series of formation periods, marked by liturgical rites celebrated at various times, might become normative for the Roman Rite.

In observance of these decrees, the Vatican Congregation for Divine Worship (CDW) prepared a new rite, approved by Pope Paul VI, for the Christian initiation of adults. The congregation declared this edition as the *typical edition*, dated January 6, 1972, to replace the earlier rite of baptism of adults found in the Roman Ritual.

In 1974, the English translation of the Rite of Christian Initiation of Adults (RCIA) was completed by the International Commission on English in the Liturgy (ICEL) and was promulgated as the *provisional text* by the United States Catholic Conference (USCC).

In 1985, after 11 years of pastoral experience, experimentation and work on the text, ICEL concluded that the time was right to progress to the "white book" stage (the temporary revised edition leading more immediately to the final version). This was published jointly by ICEL and a Commission of Catholic Bishops' Conferences in January of 1986. It included new translations of the older texts and a better ordering of introductions and rites.

In November of 1986, the National Conference of Catholic Bishops (NCCB) approved this revised book. At the same time, because of special pastoral needs, the bishops approved also a series of additions, many of which provide rites for baptized and unbaptized candidates. These were prepared by a special subcommittee of the Bishops' Committee on the Liturgy (BCL).

This entire work was confirmed for use in dioceses of the United States by the CDW in February of 1988. The date for mandatory implementation was set by the BCL for September 1, 1988. After that date, each parish in the United States is expected to have an active catechumenate and to observe the structures and rites of the RCIA. We have a text.

What Is a Commentary?

The commentaries in this book are drawn from *Catechumenate: A Journal of Christian Initiation.* They will be supplemented in *Catechumenate* and in subsequent volumes of this series.

A commentary is a guide or manual, usually in sequential order, written to aid in the interpretation of a text. Within that broad description commentaries vary a great deal.

Some commentaries emphasize one facet; others highlight another. For example, a liturgical commentator may approach a text from the perspective of two or three of the following: a) history, b) biblical images, c) theology, d) christology, e) ecclesiology, f) soteriology, g) doctrine, h) liturgy, i) the behavioral sciences, j) spirituality, k) social issues, l) structure, m) textual hermeneutic, n) a hermeneutic of human existence, o) *explication du texte*, p) linguistics, q) pastoral concerns. In the past 15 years structural and behavioral approaches have become prominent in commentaries on liturgical rites and biblical texts. Perhaps the key advice for the reader is to determine as quickly as possible in an article what methodological approach the author is using.

Long before a particular catechumenal rite, everyone responsible for some aspect of the rite should read the suitable commentary *along with the text of the rite.* Only after that should meetings be held to prepare the liturgy. The insights afforded by the commentaries in this book are intended to open up possibilities and to give presiders, musicians and other ministers insight into the rites themselves. This sort of study, constructive criticism and reflection should

2

go on every year. The rites, especially those prepared for dioceses in the United States, are themselves in need of continuing evaluation leading to eventual revision.

Can You Share Your Experience?

Could we ask you a favor? As you celebrate the rites of initiation in your parish or diocese, we would appreciate your reflections. How did you celebrate a certain part of the rite? How did it flow? What were the comments afterward? How did it enhance (or fail to enhance) the expression of the mystery? Do you have questions about it? Share your thoughts with us and we will facilitate sharing them with others. With your name and address (so that we can discuss the findings with you), contact:

> James A. Wilde, Editor
> Liturgy Training Publications
> 1800 North Hermitage Avenue
> Chicago IL 60622
> 312/486-8970

1

Acceptance into the Order of Catechumens

Richard N. Fragomeni

She had been asking all the important questions, having first entered into conversation with Mary many months ago. Reaching deeply into the possibility of starting life anew, she discovered that her old patterns of living no longer satisfied. She decided, after eight months of inquiry about the way Christians live and understand life, to take seriously the invitation of those she now calls her friends and to become a catechumen. Her name is Sally. She is the neighbor down the street, the cashier at the Giant Food Market, the woman you occasionally notice in the laundromat. You do recognize her, don't you?

She met Mary at a school board meeting last winter—by chance, she thought. They talked that evening and had coffee the next day. Mary invited her to a gathering of people the following week where Sally found others, like herself, asking questions that sting the heart, questions that do not find answers in books or on the television. And so every week for these past eight months, Sally attended sessions of inquiry and hospitality at Joe Moriarty's house. They shared stories and were given a chance to be heard. The meaning and the message of Jesus were the foundation of these experiences at Joe's house.

Richard N. Fragomeni, a priest of the diocese of Albany and former director of its Office for Liturgy, is currently completing doctoral studies in liturgy at the Catholic University of America.

And now Sally is ready. She has decided to continue her passage into Christian discipleship. For Sally, the time has come to be counted as one on the way. The parish community, therefore, will formally and compassionately accept her into a new relationship next Sunday. She will enter the catechumenate, a time and a place where she will be nourished more fully on the stories of God.

Sunday will mark the threshold into a great adventure. The adventure finds its direction in a community of the disciples of the One who died and lives. Sally has experienced the hospitality and support of our community at Joe and Jennifer Moriarty's house, and now will be given an opportunity to experience the embrace of the entire parish as she expresses her promise to follow Christ and her decision to enter the catechumenate of our parish next Sunday. Won't you be there?

The above paragraph could be a bulletin announcement in any of the parishes throughout North America that are engaged in the implementation of the Rite of Christian Initiation of Adults (RCIA). The announcement reflects Sally's questions, asked during her journey through the period of inquiry. It is an invitation to the entire parish to be aware of Sally's journey and an invitation to the community to be present at the rite of acceptance into the order of catechumens.

What will the parish liturgical assembly do to celebrate this threshold experience with Sally? How will the liturgy next Sunday express the turning point to all who journey into conversion and into the adventure of Christian praxis?

In this essay, we will set out to answer these questions. First, we will briefly examine the Rite of Acceptance into the Order of Catechumens, as approved by the bishops of the United States. Second, we will comment on some theological, liturgical and pastoral implications of the rite, giving special attention to the adaptations of the celebration, such as one might experience next Sunday at Sally's parish.

A Look at the Rite

The RCIA outlines the Rite of Acceptance into the Order of Catechumens as follows: Receiving the Candidates, Liturgy of the Word and, after the catechumens are dismissed, Liturgy of the Eucharist.

When the inquirers, their sponsors and a group of the faithful have assembled, either outside or inside the entrance of the building, the celebration begins with a song as the presider goes to greet them. The presider offers a general orientation to the celebration by recalling for the sponsors and the assembly the spiritual journey that the inquirers have been traveling. This assumes, needless to say, that the presider has been involved in the lives of the inquirers before this public celebration.

The sponsors and inquirers are invited to come forward, and the presider introduces the inquirers to the assembly, unless, of course, they are already known by the community. With questions to the inquirers, the presider ascertains their desire to continue on the journey begun during the time of inquiry. Then they are asked to make a public promise to accept the gospel and to live the Christian life as catechumens.

The sponsors and the assembly are asked to pledge their support of the inquirers by good example and by living testimony to the gospel. The presider then prays a short blessing:

> Father of mercy,
> we thank you for these your servants.
> You have sought and summoned them in many ways
> and they have turned to seek you.
>
> You have called them today
> and they have answered in our presence:
> we praise you, Lord, and we bless you.

The assembly responds: "We praise you, Lord, and we bless you," repeating the last line of the presidential prayer.

The inquirers are signed with the cross on the forehead by the presider, the sponsor and the catechist. This initial signing may be followed by the signing of the other senses. The sponsors or catechists do this signing while the presider gives language to the gesture and the assembly sings acclamations of praise. A prayer concludes the signing with the words:

> Almighty God,
> by the cross and resurrection of your Son
> you have given life to your people.
> Your servants have received the sign of the cross:
> make them living proof of its saving power
> and help them to persevere in the footsteps of Christ.

Paragraphs 58 and 59 of the rite offer two options: a new name may be given to the candidate, and the invitation to the celebration of the word of God may be preceded or followed by other gestures that signify reception into the community.

Finally, the invitation is given to the catechumens, their sponsors and the group of the faithful gathered outside of the church building to enter for the proclamation of the scriptures. The rite gives this example for the invitation: "N. and N., come into the church, to share with us at the table of God's word." All enter the building, singing a song or a psalm.

When the assembly is seated, the presider gives a brief orientation to the catechumens about the dignity of scripture in the Christian assembly. The lectionary or Bible is honored, and the liturgy of the word follows.

Paragraph 62 states that any of the readings in the lectionary that are suited for the new catechumens may be proclaimed at the celebration. Two readings from the section of ritual Masses are suggested: Genesis 12:1–4a, the call of Abraham and Sarah, and John 1:35–42, the call of the first disciples. A homily integrates the readings with the meaning of the catechumens' promise to follow Christ.

The presentation of the Bible may come after the homily. The RCIA offers no formula for this action. If the Bible is presented, the gestures for doing so must be homemade.

The assembly is invited to pray for the catechumens. These intercessions are for the candidates and their needs on the journey, including petitions for the sponsors and the catechists. The general intercessions are prayed by the assembly *after* the dismissal of the catechumens. If, in accord with paragraph 68, the general intercessions are to be omitted and the liturgy of the eucharist is to begin immediately after the dismissal of the candidates, then intentions for the church and the world may be added to the intercessions for the catechumens. A concluding prayer is led by the presider with hands outstretched over the catechumens, and they are dismissed from the assembly to continue the celebration together, sharing the joy of the experience with one another and breaking open the word that has been proclaimed. "Catechumens, go in peace, and may the Lord remain with you always!"

The Theology

The rite is situated between the periods of inquiry and catechumenate. As such, it functions as a portal to the period of formation wherein the catechumen is nourished by the great stories of tradition and is formed as a disciple of light. It is a rite of initiation to the table of the word and a moment on the journey that clarifies the meaning of Christian discipleship. This discipleship, the following of Christ and the values imaged in the gospels, is the heart of conversion.

The rite is centered around the inquirer's initial promise to follow the call of the gospel. During the entire period of inquiry, the candidate has asked questions of the meaning of life and now has come to find true meaning in the discipleship of the community of Christ. This first promise is made within the assembly of disciples who are vowed by reason of their baptismal covenant to follow Jesus.

The rite affirms the significance of the promise of the inquirer by placing immediately after it the promise of the sponsors and the entire assembly to support the new catechumens. It seems that the rite is essentially about promise making and promise keeping. It is a celebration of hospitable support and acceptance into a community of vowed Christians. Catechumens and the baptized together are engaged in announcing their involvement in the great adventure of testimony to Christ.

The promise, if seen as central to this rite, finds two rituals that give focus to its meaning. First, when Christians undertake to follow the Living One, the path leads to the cross. To keep the memory of Christ alive—at times a dangerous enterprise—the whole community is absorbed in the mystery of Christ's death. Catechumens receive the sign of the cross on their entire bodies, being marked with the magnitude of Christ's love and the immensity of Christ's pain, as a reminder of where the journey of initiation into Christ is leading. The disciples are not promised a rose garden or some middle-class success. Rather, their "blessed assurance" is a road that leads to Calvary and immersion in the Blood of the Lamb.

Second, the presentation of the scriptures seals the meaning of the first promise for the catechumens. The energy for the journey comes from the word. Catechumens are to be involved intimately with the word; it is the orientation of the period into which they now are entering. They are to read the word, devour the word and ultimately *become* the word.

The rite is frightening because when celebrated well it calls the community to the arduous task of discipleship and to the ultimate vocation of being alive in Christ for the transformation of the cosmos. It is into such a commitment and into such a community that the inquirers are being initiated. They enter the great period of formation with the promise, with the cross and with the word.

The Liturgy

The Rite of Acceptance exhibits an inconsistency of ritual pattern. In the revision of the liturgical rites, the Constitution on the Sacred Liturgy, #24, gives the following principle:

> It is from the scriptures that actions and signs derive their
> meaning. Thus to achieve the reform, progess and adaptation
> of the liturgy, it is essential to promote that warm and living
> love for scripture to which the venerable tradition of both East-
> ern and Western rites gives testimony.

The eucharistic liturgy emerges from a proclamation of the scriptures. But the Rite of Acceptance does not operate from this principle, as, for example, the sacrament of matrimony does. Evidently, those who designed the liturgy tried to make the ritual at the doorway of the church the formal initiation to the word. So the promise to follow Christ and the signing with the cross take place before the proclamation of the word. One wonders what meaning the promise or the signing of the senses can have before the proclamation of the scripture.

What if the rite were designed so that the gathering at the entrance of the church building had as its orientation a welcoming of the candidates and a formal declaration of their intentions? This gathering would be a sign of hospitality to the catechumens and a public invitation from the community to join in the hearing of the word.

After the readings and the homily, the candidates would be asked to respond to the word in promise and then be signed with the cross and given the Bible to seal the meaning of the initial commitment. The signing of the other senses and the presentation of the scriptures wouldn't be optional rites but necessary responses of the community to the catechumens' first promise.

To this author, after working with the rite for ten years, the beginning of the rite seems too abrupt, especially for a community that may not have yet taken seriously its role in the initiation of Christians. It seems more conducive to the meaning of the rite first to gather the assembly of the baptized for an orientation to the celebration and their role in it with some prayer and song. This orientation could lead into a procession of the entire community, or of those who are able, to greet the candidates with their sponsors at the front doorway or outside the church in a suitable place.

Paragraph 42 concludes with the words: "The candidates should also be instructed about the celebration of the liturgical rite of acceptance." The word "instructed" is a slippery word for people involved in liturgy. Does it mean the candidate is told what to do and where to stand and what to expect? Or does it mean that we give instruction about what the rite is all about? Or does it mean that the Rite of Acceptance is the only instruction necessary for the candidate? That the best catechesis is liturgical and the best liturgy is catechetical becomes an operating principle for those involved with the planning of the rite.

Too much instruction kills the meaning of the liturgy by defining meaning and by not allowing the imagination to soar in the varied meanings of the symbols. Certainly, sponsors should be informed of the logistics of the rite and the candidates be given the necessary formation concerning the importance of the promise that they will make. But an extended instruction about the rite undermines the meaning that can emerge in the surprise of the unfolding ritual. We must trust our symbols to have tongues and to speak for themselves. Take a chance. Leave something to the Spirit.

Pastoral Possibilities

Pastorally, acceptance into the order of catechumens is a jewel box of possibilities. Let us conclude our considerations in this essay by taking a look at three of them.

1. Do not underestimate the power of a parade. Liturgical processions are called for in the rite. Allow them to speak of the journey that the community travels together with the catechumens. If a parish gathers the assembly of the baptized before going to meet the candidates, a procession can become a living embrace of the inquirers,

11

as the community emerges out of the doors of the church to surround the candidates like a womb.

But processions are dead without song. An antiphon, well constructed in text and musical setting, can be sung by the assembly and led by cantor or choir. It can be simple enough that participation aids would not be necessary. Hands are then free for applause and embraces, which enhance the hospitality of the rite. This procession of welcome has proven to be a great sign of support for the candidates, a visual and tactile icon of God's support.

The procession back into the church for the liturgy of the word can use the same musical accompaniment. Sponsors with arms around the shoulders of the candidates can lead the candidates to their places in the church. (The sponsors are rehearsed and the candidates are advised to trust their sponsors.)

Try seeing this welcome as an opportunity for the parish to act in solidarity to express welcome and hospitality. No doubt each parish will have difficulties to overcome in creating the procession and the atmosphere of welcome. But it works. And it is important.

2. A second pastoral consideration is the placement of the candidates during the celebration of the word. Know your space and use it to speak proximity and participation. For example, if a parish community decides that the first promise and the explanatory rites should take place following the proclamation of the scriptures, then the candidates and their sponsors should be in view of the assembly for the readings.

For the first promise they remain in their positions. During the signing of the senses they can be brought down the central aisle of the church. The entire assembly can extend their hands over the candidates as the sponsors sign each of the parts of the body. One adaptation of the signing of the senses is the signing of the cross on the feet of the candidates, which now is to be found in the United States additions, with the invocation: "Receive the sign of the cross on your feet. How beautiful the feet of those who proclaim the gospel of peace!" A sung acclamation after each invocation creates still another image of interconnection and support. In any case, pastoral adaptation of the rite demands sensitivity to space and the tenor of experience that it creates.

3. What do we do when the inquirers include both the unbaptized

as well as those already baptized in another Christian tradition? Many parishes find themselves asking this question.

From the catechetical point of view, this situation is not problematic. Those who enter the process of conversion, regardless of baptismal status, can and do embark on similar journeys of the heart. What becomes problematic is the liturgical finesse that a community must use in the celebration of the rituals that mark the stages of conversion and the thresholds from one period of catechesis to another. Some parishes have solved this dilemma by separating the two groups and creating new celebration patterns for the already baptized.

A pastoral solution finds a parish celebrating the rite with both groups at the same celebration, carefully wedding the two groups in a common liturgical experience. This is done in such a way as to keep the two groups distinguished by differences in language and in seating arrangement. As long as respect is given to both groups and to the commitment of those already baptized, this option can prove viable.

This option also respects the emotional bonds forged by the group during the period of inquiry. Such group connections become part of the total liturgical experience and form the basis of an alternative way of celebrating the rite. Pastorally, distinguishing these two groups for the sake of canonical clarity does not necessitate separating catechumens and the already baptized, like sheep and goats. In all cases, acceptance into the order of catechumens must be re-created with imagination and enthusiasm, bearing in mind the people involved and the challenge of the season in which this rite is celebrated.

Sally and four other inquirers were brought into the catechumenate last Sunday. Those who shared in the celebration with our candidates were challenged by their willingness to answer the call of Christ. It is the sincere commitment of people like Sally and the others that will bring the reign of God to bear in human affairs. Sally, may God bring to completion in you what has been begun in our hearing today.

2

Anointing with
the Oil of
Catechumens

Gerard Austin

When the *Constitution on the Sacred Liturgy* of Vatican II mandated the restoration of the catechumenate, it seemed to speak of the catechumenate primarily as a period of instruction, which might secondarily possess certain ritual elements: "The catechumenate for adults, comprising several distinct steps, is to be restored and brought into use at the discretion of the local ordinary. By this means the time of the catechumenate, which is intended as a period of suitable instruction, may be sanctified by sacred rites to be celebrated at successive intervals of time" (#64). However, the council grew in its grasp of the heart of the catechumenate, as a year later in the *Decree on the Church's Missionary Activity* the emphasis was less on instruction and more on the ritual aspect:

> Those who have received from God the gift of faith in Christ, through the Church, should be admitted with liturgical rites to the catechumenate which is not a mere exposition of dogmatic truths and norms of morality but a period of formation in the whole Christian life, an apprenticeship of sufficient duration, during which the disciples will be joined to Christ their

Gerard Austin, OP, director of the Liturgical Studies Program and associate professor of theology at the Catholic University of America, is the author of *Anointing with the Spirit: The Rite of Confirmation* (New York: Pueblo, 1985).

teacher. The catechumens should be properly initiated into the mystery of salvation and the practice of the evangelical virtues, and they should be introduced into the life of faith, liturgy and charity of the people of God by successive sacred rites. (#14)

One of those "successive sacred rites" which signifies and effects that formation into the whole Christian life, and one which up until now has not received a great deal of attention, is the anointing with the oil of catechumens.

Immediate Background

When the Rite of Baptism for Children appeared in 1969, one of the adaptations left up to conferences of bishops was whether or not the anointing on the breast with the oil of catechumens could be omitted. The U.S. bishops determined, "The prebaptismal anointing with the oil of catechumens may be omitted only when the minister of baptism judges the omission to be pastorally necessary or desirable." One hoped that its omission would not be based simply upon a desire for a speedy ceremony. When the anointing with the oil of catechumens was used, the symbolic dimension was that of strength. The presider was to anoint the child on the breast, praying, "We anoint you with the oil of salvation in the name of Christ our savior; may he strengthen you with his power, who lives and reigns for ever and ever." This was a new formula, bringing out more clearly the "strengthening" dimension. The previous formula had merely stated: "I anoint you with the oil of salvation in Christ Jesus our Lord, so that you may have everlasting life." The new rite made it clear that the anointing with the oil of catechumens was to be understood in the context of the prayer of exorcism immediately preceding the anointing. Indeed, the exorcism determined the meaning of the anointing. The exorcism underscored the state of evil in the world into which the child was born; the anointing with the oil of catechumens offered a remedy for the evil—namely, the strength of Christ.

Three years later, in 1972, the adult rite appeared in Latin, but it was not until 1974 that it was available in English: *Rite of Christian Initiation of Adults* (Provisional Text). Anointing with the oil of catechumens in the adult rite appeared twice: as an optional rite during the catechumenate (#103, #127–132) and as part of the celebration of the sacraments of initiation during the Easter Vigil (#218). This latter usage could be applied on Holy Saturday "if it cannot be done during the Easter Vigil because of lack of time" (#202). The anointing during the catechumenate was not highly stressed or explained. The text simply stated, "According to local usage and desire, celebration may be provided for the rite of anointing with the oil of catechumens" (#103). Just as in the rite of baptism for children, the anointing was meant to strengthen the catechumens. As expressed in the case of its usage at the Easter Vigil, "It should signify the need of God's strength so that the person who is being baptized, despite the bonds of his past life and overcoming of adversity of the devil, strongly takes the step of professing his faith and holds to it without faltering throughout his entire life" (#212). It was to take place at the end of the celebration of the word of God and was to be given to all the catechumens, although "for special reasons it may also be given privately to individuals" (#128). It was also permitted to anoint the catechumens several times, if this was thought desirable (#128). The anointing was "on the breast or on both hands or even on other parts of the body" (#130), and the formula to be used was the new one quoted above for the rite of baptism for children. That same formula was used both during the catechumenate (#130) and during the Easter Vigil (#218) or, if anticipated, on Holy Saturday.

During the years that followed the promulgation of the RCIA, it would not be an understatement to say that, in the United States anyway, the anointing with the oil of catechumens was not the most popular or most discussed feature of the new rite. In some places it was used for the rite of becoming catechumens along with the signing of the cross on the forehead. Certain places in Africa reported its repeated usage at different stages of progress during the catechumens' journey.

Revised Text

In November of 1986 the National Conference of Catholic Bishops approved the revised text of the RCIA. This edition incorporated the emendations of the text necessitated by the new Code of Canon Law. Furthermore, the bishops approved 11 ritual determinations, two of which had to do with the anointing with the oil of catechumens:

Number Seven: "Does the National Conference of Catholic Bishops approve the use of the anointing with the oil of catechumens during the period of the catechumenate as a kind of 'rite of passage'?" The vote was affirmative.

Number Nine: "Does the National Conference of Catholic Bishops approve the reserving of the anointing with the oil of catechumens to the period of the catechumenate and to the period of purification and enlightenment, and approve omitting it in the preparation rites on Holy Saturday and in the celebration of initiation at the Easter Vigil or at another time?" Again, the vote was affirmative. Thus, the RCIA additions for the dioceses of the U.S. present the anointing with the oil of catechumens, not as a ritual for the Easter Vigil (or if anticipated, for Holy Saturday), but as a repeatable rite to be used during the catechumenate itself, that is, during the period of the catechumenate or during the period of purification and enlightenment.

This decision seems to be a good one. The "strengthening" element pertains more to the process of the catechumenate than to the moment of the giving of the initiation sacraments at the Easter Vigil. (Note: I am using "catechumenate" in the broad sense to include both the period of the catechumenate and the period of purification and enlightenment.) Many feel that the catechumenate is ritually weak. Adding this anointing, especially at repeated junctures, should help express ritually the strength the catechumens receive from Christ to battle against the forces of evil.

Use of Oil

The ritual use of oil in the early church was greatly influenced by the pagan and secular use of oil in antiquity and by the typologies of the Hebrew Scriptures. In the bath, oil held the place that soap does in modern life, and in the gymnasium athletes freely oiled themselves for games and exercises. In the religious sphere, these usages of health and sport were often paralleled, especially in conjunction with sacrifice. Leonel L. Mitchell puts the matter well in his book *Baptismal Anointing*:

> We can see the importance which oil had in the life of the average Roman. Not only did he cook with it, burn it in his lamps and wash with it, but he used it as a medicine, as a cosmetic and in religious rites. The association of washing and anointing was extremely close both in religious ceremonial and

18

> in daily life. Certainly the idea of a sacred anointing would not
> have been alien to the mind of a neophyte coming to the church
> from the pagan Roman world. (p. 28)

In the Hebrew Scriptures oil was used for both things and persons. Jacob poured oil over the stone at Bethel (Genesis 28:18); a warrior's shield might be anointed (Isaiah 21:5). Most important, oil was used in anointing kings (1 Samuel 10:1; 16:13; 2 Kings 9:6; 11:12; 23:30), prophets (1 Kings 19:16; Isaiah 61:1–2) and priests (Exodus 28:41; 29:7; Leviticus 8:12; Numbers 3:3). The anointing makes the king or priest a sacred person, the "anointed of the Lord," which in Hebrew is "the Messiah" and in Greek "the Christ."

The most important source of information for the use of oil in the early baptismal ceremonies is the *Apostolic Tradition* of Hippolytus, written around the year 215. Here we find two kinds of oil: "oil of exorcism" which the bishop has exorcised, and "oil of thanksgiving" over which he has given thanks. The "oil of exorcism" was used before baptism (as we use the oil of catechumens today) and the "oil of thanksgiving" was used after baptism (as we use chrism today). Our concern here is the first anointing. Before the water rite in the *Apostolic Tradition* a presbyter anoints saying, "May every evil spirit depart from you." Thus, the prebaptismal anointing was clearly in the context of an exorcism. This was to be the hallmark of the Roman tradition. Let me again quote Leonel Mitchell in his *Baptismal Anointing*, for he summarizes so well:

> Baptism is preceded by an anointing with exorcised oil. In
> *Apostolic Tradition* the whole body was anointed. John the
> Deacon speaks of anointing the ears, the nostrils and the breast.
> The Roman liturgical books know only the anointing of the breast
> and back. The trend is to reduce the amount of oil used. Anoint-
> ings become signings with the cross on selected, symbolic mem-
> bers of the body. The meaning, nevertheless, remains unchanged.
> It is an exorcism guarding the body of the catechumen from the
> attack of the devil so that it may become a temple of the Holy
> Ghost. (p. 169)

The problem was that other places in the West, especially Gaul, forgot this Roman tradition and confused the oil of catechumens with chrism, ultimately turning the oil of catechumens into a type of "second-class chrism." This was a major factor in the loss of a sense of importance for the ritual role played by the oil of catechumens.

The New Rite

Today the rite of anointing with the oil of catechumens is again well grounded in the context of exorcism. The blessing of oils gives the key principle for understanding the use of the oil of catechumens: "By the oil of catechumens the effect of the baptismal exorcisms is extended" (Rite of the Blessing of Oils [RBO], #2). To understand the correct role of the anointing with the oil of catechumens, then, one must understand the correct role of a baptismal exorcism. Perhaps the key thing to remember is that no exorcism is purely negative. To put it another way, two spirits are involved in an exorcism: the evil spirit and the Holy Spirit. The evil spirit is forced out to the extent that the Holy Spirit takes over the life of the candidate. The whole catechumenal process is an encounter with a Spirit-filled community; the Holy Spirit rubs off on the catechumens because they are "rubbing shoulders" with a Spirit-filled community. That is why no exorcism is totally negative; that is why historically the use of the anointing with the oil of catechumens reveals both an exorcistic-healing motif and a union-with-Christ motif.

In light of this, one is somewhat disappointed with the blessing prayer for the oil of catechumens, which was the work of the committee entrusted with the reform of the initiation rite: "Lord God, protector of all who believe in you, bless this oil and give wisdom and strength to all who are anointed with it in preparation for their baptism. Bring them to a deeper understanding of the gospel, help them to accept the challenge of Christian living, and lead them to the joy of new birth in the family of your church. We ask this through Christ our Lord. Amen." (RBO, #22). Perhaps the phrase "help them to accept the challenge of Christian living" could have been more forcefully expressed to bring out the concrete evils against which the candidates need to be strengthened: evils of egoism, violence, injustice.

The oil of catechumens was traditionally blessed in the Roman liturgy by a bishop in the context of the eucharist, after the communion rite. At first it was done at the Easter Vigil, but by the sixth century this action had been transferred to Holy Thursday, probably to lighten the Easter Vigil ceremonies. Today, the Rite of the Blessing of Oils states: "If the use of the oil of catechumens is retained by the conference of bishops, it is blessed by the bishop with the other oils during the chrism Mass. In the case of baptism of adults, however, priests have the faculty to bless the oil of catechumens before the anointing in the designated stage of the catechumenate" (RBO, #7). It should be noted that the Eastern practice has been for the priest to bless the oil at the time it is to be used.

Who Should Anoint?

The answer to this question is best determined when we recall the overall context for the use of the oil of catechumens during the catechumenate. The anointing takes place in the context of celebrations of the word of God. The ICEL text of the RCIA explains:

> During the period of the catechumenate there should be celebrations of the word of God that accord with the liturgical season and that contribute to the instruction of the catechumens and the needs of the community. These celebrations of the word are: first, celebrations held specially for the catechumens; second, participation in the liturgy of the word at the Sunday Mass; third, celebrations held in connection with catechetical instruction. (#81)

The sequence proposed for these celebrations is song, readings and responsorial psalms, homily, concluding rites of minor exorcism, blessing, anointing (#85–89).

Both the frequency of these celebrations and their precise form will best be determined by someone who is very close to the life and struggle of the catechumens. It would seem that the catechists best fit this bill. They would be the most competent to judge just who needs to be strengthened and when. While we may want to preserve the tradition of the oil itself being blessed by a bishop or a priest, the use of the oil is a different matter. It would seem that the catechists would be in the best position to lead the catechetical instruction and bring it to its completion with the ritual of minor exorcism, blessing and, at certain times, anointing with the oil of catechumens. The argument finds a parallel in Hippolytus' *Apostolic Tradition* where it was the catechist who imposed hands and blessed the catechumens after each catechetical instruction (Book 2:19). The present legislation allows catechists to be deputed by the bishop to perform the minor exorcisms and blessings (#16), but the rite of anointing with the oil of catechumens is reserved to a priest or deacon (#98). Would it not be better for the same minister to preside over the entire celebration, including the anointing with the oil of catechumens?

The frequency of anointing will vary a great deal according to needs. Catechesis based on the lectionary will bring to the surface a great number of issues. It will invite the catechumens to look at a lot of things in their lives. Ritual expressions of the strength of Christ will be needed to help them carry out Jesus' commands in their lives. A frequent and a good example is the scriptural lesson of the need for compassion and forgiveness. Catechumens are frequently blessed with new insights in this area, and they want and need to ritualize this by purging any former hardness of heart and being anointed with the strength of Christ to walk "the extra mile."

The tactility of the anointing with the oil of catechumens is an important element. It serves as a marvelous means of binding the catechumens to the community. One sees the wisdom of the fourth-century practices as described by St. Cyril of Jerusalem: "Next, after removing your garments you were rubbed with exorcised oil from the hair of your head to your toes, and so you became sharers in Jesus Christ, who is the cultivated olive tree" *(Mystagogical Catechesis,* 2:3). Catechumens often feel isolated. They need to be strengthened, encouraged—in a word, touched. In this sense the repeated anointing with the oil of catechumens would be seen as a harbinger of the kiss of peace to be received in the Easter Vigil.

Elements Involved

As mentioned above, the anointing with the oil of catechumens is now to be found as one of the elements of the concluding rites of the "Celebrations of the Word of God" which take place during the period of the catechumenate. The elements of the concluding rites are three: minor exorcism, blessing of the catechumens, anointing of the catechumens. For the interrelationship of these three elements, #89 of the RCIA text is important: "Concluding Rites: The celebration of the word may conclude with a minor exorcism (#94) or with a blessing of the catechumens (#97). When the minor exorcism is used, it may be followed by one of the blessings (#97) or, on occasion, by the rite of anointing" (#102–103).

The wording here is precise and important. The anointing with the oil of catechumens is envisioned as a more common occurrence than it has been in the past, still, not to the extent that it would be used at every celebration of the word during the catechumenate. On the other hand, every time the anointing is used, it should be preceded by a minor exorcism. This is important to ensure the proper context for the use of the oil of catechumens, that is, the context of exorcism.

The minor exorcisms "have been composed in the form of petitions directly addressed to God. They draw the attention of the catechumens to the real nature of Christian life, the struggle between flesh and spirit, the importance of self-denial for reaching the blessedness of God's kingdom, and the unending need for God's help" (#90). It is precisely in this context that the catechumens are anointed, because their strength is to be found in Christ our savior. This is the key to understanding the rite of anointing. Christ is the source of the power that will conquer the struggles involved in the conversion process. It is precisely the spirit of Christ that will, as one of the exorcism prayers states, "protect them from the spirit of evil and guard them against error and sin" (#94).

Conclusion

This repeated and prayerful use of the oil of catechumens is something relatively unknown to most of us. It will take a while to put it to best use. In the meantime we should share our experiences with one another. The lessons of history as to the healing and strengthening powers of oil should be attended to, as well as the present experiences of charismatic Christians.

The final and most important factor in determining the use of the anointing during the catechumenate will be the word of God itself. The word of Jesus is an effective word. It is a word of power. The power (Greek, *dynamis)* is shown in a special way in the gospels when Jesus performs healings and exorcisms. "They were all amazed and said to one another, 'What is this word? For with authority and power he commands the unclean spirits, and they come out'" (Luke 4:36). For the catechumens the word of God is gradually broken open by a catechesis that stems from the lectionary. The lectionary is their main textbook. As their faith grows and develops out of this source, they will periodically be overwhelmed by their present struggles and by the path that still lies ahead of them. Through the anointing with the oil of catechumens they will be comforted, knowing that the power and strength of Christ is with them during their journey. The very word that challenges them, and at times frightens them, will provide the power *(dynamis)* that will lead them ultimately to the waters of baptism and a life in the Spirit.

3

Election or Enrollment of Names

Allan Bouley

"Election" in everyday speech refers to a kind of contest. By putting themselves forward or by nomination, persons become candidates. In the election itself votes are cast and the fate of the candidates is decided. They become winners or losers. "Election" in our new Catholic liturgical vocabulary, however, has a different meaning, and perhaps it is unfortunate that a better term has not been found to express it.

Our purpose here is to comment on that specific part of the RCIA called the Rite of Election or Enrollment of Names in order to understand the special meaning of election as a ritual in itself within the full sweep of the RCIA. The commentary deals with the rite from theological, liturgical and pastoral perspectives.

It is presumed here that the rite of election is celebrated within the eucharist at its normal time on the First Sunday of Lent (#126, #128) and that the bishop usually presides, making it an episcopal liturgy as envisioned by the RCIA (#121). Other forms of the rite, for example, the rite of election celebrated outside the eucharist, various local parish rites of sending or election as well as rites for calling already baptized persons to continuing conversion in the church or to communion with it, will be discussed in other chapters

---

Allan Bouley, OSB, is a monk of St. John's Abbey and professor of liturgical studies and pastoral liturgy at St. John's University, Collegeville, Minnesota.

of this book and in future issues of *Catechumenate: A Journal of Christian Initiation.*

Introducing the Rites

As the liturgy begins on the First Sunday of Lent, it is important that the presence of catechumens and their sponsors and of all candidates for election and their godparents be acknowledged. The fact that election and enrollment will take place needs to be stated. The assembly of the faithful should be invited to participate fully, not as mere spectators of what happens to others but as members of the community of the church, chosen by God in baptism and entering into the lenten season with the catechumens for the sake of renewed conversion and baptismal commitment.

Especially where the RCIA is a new experience, all this needs to be done. The rite of election should not simply happen out of the blue once the homily is over, but the entire assembly should be led into that event as an integral part of the Sunday's liturgy, which is shaped from beginning to end by the rite of election.

Liturgy of the Word

The scriptural lessons of any of the three cycles for this Sunday are appropriate for the celebration of election, but those of Cycle A are perhaps most suitable and accessible. Genesis 3–4 places the fact of sin and alienation from God squarely in human history and upon the shoulders of willful humanity by telling the story of the fall of Adam and Eve. The Adam/Christ contrast (Romans 5) proclaims the good news that sin and death have been radically overcome by the free gift of God's grace in Jesus Christ. The gospel (Matthew 4:1–11) establishes the 40-day fast of Jesus as a paradigm for the community's lenten observance and recounts the triple temptation of Jesus: The most devious allurements the darkness of this world can offer are rebuffed by him whose sustenance, mission and power rest in God alone.

Thus the full drama of sin and redemption is set out in all its woe and glory so that it can echo in the experience of the catechumens and faithful. The very pattern and possibility of lifelong and lenten conversion rest in the faithful following of Jesus who calls us to a life graced by the free gift of God. The homily must relate this age-old drama to the present lives of catechumens and faithful alike (#129).

Rite of Election
or Enrollment of Names

The rite occurs after the homily (#130). The title of the rite, Election or Enrollment of Names, seems odd. It is not a question here of one *or* the other, nor is one the *same* as the other, as though the names and the actions were interchangeable. The rite comprises the church's act of election *and* the catechumens' act of giving and enrolling their names. This minor ambiguity in the title hints at a greater lack of clarity that remains within the rite despite the changed formulas and headings of the new text. The ambiguities are more apparent if we remember that rubrics and headings are not read out loud in order to elucidate the rite as it is celebrated. Rather, the rite speaks its meaning through the words actually spoken and the actions done, and in most cases the actions speak meaning louder than words. Moving through a real or imagined "performance" of the rite as given and reflecting on its acts and words can generate some uncertainty about the meaning and the interrelationships of some of its parts.

Presentation of the Catechumens

The candidates for election are presented (#130) to the bishop as a group by an appropriate person who, speaking for them, requests eventual admission to the sacraments of initiation. The presider invites them forward, along with their godparents. What follows is confusing: The candidates and godparents are called by name. On the one hand, the RCIA obviously places some importance on this "calling" for it should be done beforehand by catechists if it cannot be done during the election because of large numbers. This importance, however, is nowhere explained. On the other hand, this act of calling by name is impressive and striking and easily confused with the act of election or with the presenting/enrollment of names, which follows later.

This initial calling, found also as an option at the beginning of the acceptance into the order of catechumens (#50), seems to function as a formal introduction of the candidates and godparents to the assembly. Possibly, this call is modeled on a similar call of candidates in the rite of ordination, a model of questionable value in the rite of election where the call's impact as action conflicts with the later and more important giving/enrolling of names. At this point in the rite, a simple presentation of all the candidates and godparents together and an invitation to them to come forward would be simpler and briefer and would eliminate confusion.

Affirmation by the Godparents
(and the Assembly)

The affirmation (#131) presumes and states two things: The candidates for election have asked for initiation at Easter; their communities have engaged in a serious process of discernment, judging their genuine desire and deciding to call them to the sacraments. The godparents, who today begin their proper function, bear witness of the community's decision (form A) or to the signs of conversion in the candidates' lives (form B). The affirmation is not merely a pro forma exchange of questions and answers. It provides strong, public attestation within the liturgical gathering of the church that God's gracious call to these catechumens has already been recognized in their communities and that today it will be sacramentally expressed by the church as a call to Easter baptism, confirmation and eucharist. The rite states that the entire assembly is asked to express its approval of the candidates "when appropriate in the circumstances" (#131). It is hard to imagine a situation where this would not be appropriate.

Invitation and Enrollment of Names

The presider speaks to the catechumens (#132), telling them [somewhat superfluously] what has just been done: "Your godparents (and this entire community) have spoken in your favor." Then, speaking for the church, he formally calls them to the Easter sacraments. The church does not call them on its own but "in the name of Christ," acknowledging that Christ's call has already been heard by them. Today, the church's call embodies in human voice the call of God to which the catechumens have responded. They then are asked to express their response here and now in the presence of the church: "Do you wish to enter fully into the life of the church through the sacraments of baptism, confirmation and the eucharist?" (#132). They respond, "We do," and are invited to offer their names for enrollment.

The giving/inscription of names translates into ritual action the catechumens' responses just made to the church's call. Its impact as action should not be minimized by merely presenting a list of their names to the bishop, unless circumstances make it absolutely necessary. The rite seems to imply that the catechumens give their names *and* inscribe them, and *both* actions are construed as a *single* response. How this is done may vary. A possible pattern: Each catechumen moves to the place of enrollment accompanied by his/her godparent(s). The catechumen announces his/her name loudly and clearly to the assembly (and perhaps also announces the name of the godparent). Then, at a handsome writing stand, lectern or small, high table in the midst of or at least facing the assembly, the catechumen writes his/her name in the Book of the Elect, and the godparent does the same.

An alternate pattern for these actions would see them as a repetition of the call/response dynamic previously expressed in words. In this pattern each catechumen is *called* by name loudly and clearly (preferably by a catechist from the candidate's own community). Then the catechumen *responds* by moving forward with godparent(s) for the inscription of names as above. In either case, a previous calling by name at the beginning of the rite seems confusing and redundant. If the names are announced or called aloud they should not be made inaudible by music during the enrollment (the rite suggests Psalm 16) no matter how long it takes. Instead, an acclamation should be sung after each name if they are few, after a group of names (e.g., from a given parish) or at the end of the enrollment when they are many.

Sometimes the enrollment is done with the book placed on the altar table or held in the lap of the presider. Neither arrangement seems to be a good idea. Catechumens are still liminal people and do not participate fully in the meal-sacrifice of the church; their place is not at the altar. Though tradition has recognized the altar as a symbol of Christ, this bit of arcane knowledge does not seem widespread today among the people who themselves, in liturgical assembly, are a living sign of Christ's presence. Enrollment in the midst of Christ's living body is a better sign than inscription at the altar, which, in any case, should not be made into a writing table. The role of the presiding bishop (pastor) is important, for he teaches, speaks, prays and leads as a sign of and in ministry to the local, diocesan church. Nevertheless, the catechumens' responses are not made to him personally and should not look like it is. Kneeling at his feet to sign a book in his lap gives this impression. It is a kind of feudal gesture (borrowed

29

unconsciously from ordination rites?) little suited to our culture. Besides that, it entails assuming a posture difficult or impossible for many elderly or handicapped persons and probably repugnant for women of even mild feminist sensibility.

Act of Admission or Election

The new version of the rite improves upon the old at least to the extent of making it much clearer that this is the moment of formal election (#133): "N. and N., I now declare you to be members of the elect, to be initiated into the sacred mysteries at the next Easter Vigil." The statement is performative: It accomplishes what it says. Up to this point, the persons involved have been called candidates or catechumens; from this moment they are also called or referred to as the elect or the chosen. The ritual pattern here seems to make good sense: The catechumens have heard God's call through the voice of the church; they have responded in the act of enrollment; now their election is solemnly affirmed. Thus the liturgy also ritualizes and celebrates what has been happening in their lives as catechumens and provides a pivot point for their immediate future. The moment of turning is the bishop's statement that they are numbered among the elect. They receive new status, duties and opportunities as they enter the lenten time of purification and enlightenment leading them toward the mother of all vigils when faith, water, oil, bread and wine will bond them in communion with God's covenant people.

With a few words the presider then commends the elect to the solicitude of their godparents who show that they receive them into their care by laying a hand on their shoulder. We may discover in the high emotion of this moment that a strong embrace is a less antiseptic gesture.

Intercessions for the Elect

Two model formularies are provided (#134). The presider's opening invitation to prayer declares: "These elect, whom we bring with us to the Easter sacraments, will look to us for an example of Christian renewal. Let us pray to the Lord for *them* and for *ourselves*." The intercessions of form A do express what the invitation leads us to expect: prayer for the church, the elect and others in our common renewal as we move toward Easter. Form B, however, is entirely a "they" formulary focused solely on the elect (with one reference to their families) and making no mention of the "ourselves" of the community. The anomalous character of this formulary should have been rectified in the current revision. In neither form A nor form B are the elect to be invited to pray along with the church.

Prayer over the Elect

It is hard to understand why this prayer (two options provided) is given a separate heading (#135) for its function is to conclude the preceding intercessions. Prayer is made explicitly for the elect and hands are extended over them, but the prayers include by allusion the whole church, indeed all of humanity.

Dismissal of the Elect

Three options are now provided (#136). In form A in the context of the eucharistic celebration, the elect are normally dismissed with these words:

> My dear elect, you have set out with us on the road that leads to the glory of Easter. Christ will be your way, your truth and your life. Until we meet again for the scrutinies, walk always in his peace.

Form B is not a dismissal at all but rather a somewhat awkward statement to the elect who cannot be sent away, reminding them that they may not receive communion but inviting them to stay:

> Although you cannot yet participate fully in the Lord's eucharist, stay with us as a sign of our hope that all God's children will eat and drink with the Lord and work with his Spirit to re-create the face of the earth.

Form C is a brief dismissal of the entire assembly when the eucharist is not celebrated—an arrangement that, it seems to me, should be avoided even at large, episcopal celebrations of election, because the fullest experience of baptismal election on the part of the community of the faithful finds its profoundest context in the eucharistic liturgy, the meal of the covenant.

Theological Reflections on the Rite

The theology expressed or implicit in the rite of election and in

31

view of its place within the whole process of the RCIA is a theology of grace, of the human person, of church and of sacrament.

The election celebrated is not a win-or-lose contest decided by votes. Election, rather, celebrates the grace of a God who saves and whose Holy Spirit has touched and guided the catechumens every step of the way from first interest in the good news to the present moment. God's gracious Spirit is always first, always sheer gift, and God's loving kindness is sure as the elect move on to baptism, to full life in the church and to the promised completion of life through death.

For God's grace to have meaning and effects in a person's life, the person's free yet graced response must sustain the dialogue. Perhaps that human response is a small glimmer of hope as God begins to be recognized in Jesus Christ. As faith deepens, it finds in Christ the pattern of human life in a world poised tensely between evil and good, sin and forgiveness, suffering and trustful endurance, death and life. The human response, brought to lively faith, hope and love by the Spirit of grace, becomes a desire for full sacramental initiation into the community of faith. Election celebrates the catechumens' response to God, authenticates their personal desire for initiation, calls each by name to the Easter sacraments, and turns their personal response into a public act signed and sealed by the church, the community of their Christian lives coming-to-be.

Election shows that the church is not some amalgam of political parties vying for office but only and astoundingly the sacrament of Christ whose Spirit is the church's life and power. Without the covenant fidelity of God, the leadership of Jesus Christ and the fullness of the Holy Spirit, the church is nothing and can accomplish nothing by way of evangelization, catechesis, election and initiation. Electing catechumens, the church humbly celebrates itself as the community of God's gifts and calls itself to renewed fidelity despite its obvious human debilities. It chooses to elect only because God has done so and in the name of Jesus Christ. It invites the elect to ever fuller participation in its work: preaching good news, prayer, asceticism, reconciliation, worship and service. All this is Christ's work visible in the community of faith for the life of the world.

Election and the entire process of the RCIA shows more lucidly than any theory of sacraments that the church's sacraments are never mere moments of automatic infusion of grace isolated from life. Like election, authentic sacraments celebrate in the church what has been going on in the lives of believers and what is at the heart of the church's life. Sacraments bring the ongoing process of the life of faith and its times of growth, crisis and transition into clear focus with word and symbol, thereby gracing, strengthening and renewing persons in the community and moving them forward with deepened faith and replenished hope. The rite of election sums up in word and symbol where the catechumens have been; it graces and heightens where they are now; it pivots them forward with paschal hope toward Easter and the promise of eternal life. Every sacrament should do the same.

Election is not a contest decided by vote. It is a free gift of God choosing persons who freely respond with faith and conversion. Elected by the church in the name of Jesus Christ, they move toward font and table, running the race of faith-filled life in the community of believers, pursuing the victory crown of everlasting life.

4

The Presentations: Creed and Lord's Prayer

Aidan Kavanagh

Other chapters in this book deal with the dispositions of the Rite of Christian Initiation of Adults for acceptance into the order of catechumens, for election to receive baptism when next it will be administered and for celebrating the Easter Vigil. Here I will say a few words about what the Rite calls the Presentations.

The presentations are nothing more nor less than the final major instructional events of the catechumenate. They regularly occur in connection with the scrutinies, which take place on later Sundays in Lent. This makes the presentations acts of *public* instruction, the only such acts that are said to be so. In other words, of all the instructions catechumens receive during their preparation for the sacraments of initiation, only the final two are to be done in public as the entire church approaches the passover of its Lord and its own passover in him. The implication is that at this point the church's catechumens have emerged as public persons: Their conversions are publicly scrutinized during Sunday liturgies; they, along with the entire assembly, are publicly instructed concerning the community's

Aidan Kavanagh, OSB, is a monk of the Archabbey of St. Meinrad, professor of liturgics and Dean of the Divinity School, Yale University. He is author of *The Shape of Baptism: The Rite of Christian Initiation* (New York: Pueblo, 1974) and of the *Confirmation: Origins and Reform* (New York: Pueblo, 1987).

ancient documents of faith (the creed) and prayer (the Lord's Prayer); then both the church and its catechumens enter Pascha hand in hand, having been reminded one last time that together they are a people of *faith* in God in Christ who *pray* as their Lord himself commanded.

What Is Presented?

The ancient Latin term for presentations is *traditiones*, which means "handings over," "traditions." This clarifies the rather ambiguous English word presentations, which may suggest to some that it is the catechumens who are being "presented" to the church. These catechumens have, however, already been presented to the church at the time of their election early in Lent. The Latin word suggests that it is not someone who is being presented socially to someone else but that some*thing* is being given or passed along to some*one*. This is clearly the sense of the Rite (#147):

> The presentations, by which the church hands on to the elect its ancient documents of faith and prayer . . . lead them to enlightenment or illumination. The profession of faith (the creed) recalls the wonderful work of God for the salvation of man; it deepens the faith and joy of the elect. In the Lord's Prayer, they acknowledge more firmly the new spirit of sonship by which they will call God their Father, especially in the midst of the congregation assembled for the eucharist.

It is the ancient documents of faith and prayer that are presented to the catechumens. And if one may be permitted to say so, this is where the disposition of the rites for the presentations may begin to mislead.

More than Documents

I say this because the Rite will likely be read by many people as emphasizing the symbol rather than what is being symbolized. The symbol is the ancient document as it is given to the catechumen. Religious publishers are even now printing creed and the Lord's Prayer texts on bond paper "suitable for framing" or laminating them in plastic for use in this liturgy. There is nothing wrong with this except that it may lead people astray from what is being symbolized. What is being symbolized here is not merely passing out ancient documents but the *teaching* of which the texts are signs. The very term *traditio*, which renders the Greek word *paradosis* often used by St. Paul, is a verbal noun that means primarily *to teach*. *Paradosis* and *traditio* name the content and the act by which a body of teaching is transmitted in whole or in part from teacher to the taught. St. Paul wrote, "I commend you because you remember me in everything and maintain the traditions [i.e., the teachings of Christ and the apostles] just as I passed them on to you" (1 Corinthians 11:2); and "So then, brethren, stand firm and hold to the traditions which I taught you" (2 Thessalonians 2:15; see also 3:b). Whenever a teacher teaches he commits an act of tradition. This is a richly complex notion that the English word presentation simplifies by flattening it out.

But the issue is more important than this, at least so far as the rite is concerned. Focusing the presentations on the giving of ancient documents to senior catechumens in #147, the rite also allows the presentations to be anticipated before the scrutinies (#104, #105) or even to be done apart from the scrutinies, ". . . after the liturgy of the word at a weekday Mass with appropriate readings for the presentations" (#157, #158, #178, #179). The Rite can therefore be read as permitting the presentations at any time late in the catechumenate (even before the act of election) or during election on any weekday following the Third and Fifth Sundays of Lent, the creed first and then the Lord's Prayer. Readings and ritual directions are given for both events.

Some Ambiguities

The policy is, paradoxically, at once clear and confusing. What is clear is that the presentations are not part of the public scrutinies on the Third and Fifth Sundays of Lent; it is said to be "desirable" that they occur at weekday Masses following these two Sundays, although they might occur even before election. What are pastors, catechists, sponsors and catechumens to conclude from this?

One conclusion might be that the ambiguity concerning a definite time and circumstance for performing the presentations indicates that they are not regarded as a vital feature of the initiatory process. This indication is stronger because of the desirability that they take place not during the scrutinies of the Third and Fifth Sundays of Lent but on weekdays following these Sundays.

Another conclusion might be that putting the presentations on a level subordinate to the scrutinies (which emphasize prayer and exorcism) is recommended because the presentations focus merely on giving "ancient documents" to the catechumens. This may have the effect of trivializing the events, the "ancient documents," and even the teaching they represent. One needs to remember that the creed is, after all, not merely an old text but a summation of the trinitarian faith which the catechumens will profess in their baptism. Nor is the Lord's Prayer merely a treasured antique but the Lord's own summation of how those who believe in him are to approach his Father, beseeching him to establish his kingdom on earth and to save all people. Both creed and prayer are perennially relevant and contemporary expressions of Christian existence: To know them is to know the church's faith in its most condensed and basic form. As such, both creed and Lord's Prayer encapsulate the whole content of the catechumens' formation for baptism spread out over several years. Far from being merely old texts, creed and prayer sum up the entirety of Christian teaching, the *traditio*, the *paradosis*, as it is being passed on to catechumens within the community called into being by that same teaching, the church. It is irreducible teaching of the faith that saves. To trivialize this in any way would be tantamount to dissolving that which binds the church in unity. The issue is thus one of paramount importance.

Egeria

One may see what this involved practically, and how seriously it was taken, in the description of catechesis in fourth-century Jerusalem given by the pilgrim Egeria, who was an eyewitness of it. The catechist is the bishop himself, and he teaches daily from his chair in the church. She writes:

> His subject is God's law; during the 40 days (of Lent) he goes through the whole Bible, beginning with Genesis, and first relating the literal meaning of each passage, then interpreting its spiritual meaning. He also teaches them at this time all about the resurrection and the faith. And this is called *catechesis*. After five weeks' teaching they receive the creed, whose content he explains article by article in the same way he explained the scriptures, first literally and then spiritually. Thus all the people in these parts are able to follow the scriptures when they are read

in church, since there has been teaching on all the scriptures from six to nine in the morning all through Lent, three hours' catechesis a day. At ordinary services when the bishop sits and preaches, . . . the faithful utter exclamations, but when they come and hear him explaining the catechesis, their exclamations are far louder, God is my witness; and when it is related and interpreted like this they ask questions on each point. *(Egeria's Travels*, ed. John Wilkinson, London, 1973, 144–45.)

This is one of the earliest mentions of catechumens "receiving the creed," and one notes that the emphasis is not on giving an "ancient document" but on expounding its content, on teaching it both to catechumens and anyone of the faithful who care to listen. One also notes the amount of time given to catechesis during Lent: three hours a day for at least 40 days, a total of 120 hours just for the elect or senior catechumens. No trivialization here. "Presentation," *traditio, paradosis*, means *teaching*, and a lot of it.

Other Traditions

This same concern can be traced in other churches later. Some of them taught their catechumens not only about the creed but also about the Lord's Prayer. Others emphasized teaching the gospels, whence came the name for elect catechumens in West Syria, "the illuminated," because "the gospels are their illumination." In Western Europe some Gallican churches seem to have taught and given Psalm 23 also to their senior catechumens—an appropriate choice because this psalm, when put on the tongue of catechumens, is almost an autobiographical description of their state of soul: serene and trusting, on the verge of their baptism, not to say a verbal icon of every Christian's life.

> The Lord rules over me; I want for nothing.
> He has made me to lie down in green pasture.
> He has given me refreshing water and converted my soul.
> He leads me in the path of justice for his name's sake.
> Even though I walk beneath the shadow of death,
> I fear nothing because you are with me.
> Your rod and staff comfort me.
> You have spread a table before me against those who afflict me.

You have anointed my head with oil:
how good is the cup that rejoices me.
And your mercy will follow me all the days of my life.
I shall dwell in the Lord's house forever.

This reminds one how consciously catechumenal and baptismal the old stratum of lenten readings for Sundays, Mondays, Wednesdays and Fridays (the original "liturgical" days of public assembly) were in the Roman system. The gospel readings emphasize Jesus' teachings of his good news to his disciples, who are symbolic of the church's catechumens being taught the same news by their preachers and catechists in preparation for their baptism. At the same time the readings from Hebrew Scriptures often present complementary images of catechumens as they overcome threats and perils to their integrity as chosen children of God—images such as those of Jonah among the sinful Ninevites, Daniel in a hostile land, Mordecai in an alien court, prophets among disbelieving people, Joseph oppressed by his reviling brothers, Jacob betrayed by Esau and protected by his mother Rebecca, Naaman the soldier afflicted with leprosy, the Israelites parched in the desert and Susanna sexually harrassed by old men, to name but a few. These lessons were not random or arbitrary selections whose purpose was to inculcate a general spirit of lenten penitence. They represent a system that was meant to mine the whole of the scriptures, Hebrew and Greek, so as to teach the entire church publicly, with God's own words, the nature and demands of its own conversion to the Word who is its Lord. This rich biblical teaching centered on those coming to faith for the first time: The church's catechumens are, in this sense, living symbols of itself in faith.

The whole system of lenten teaching, of course, culminated in rather massive readings of the Easter Vigil, which today total nine (seven from the Hebrew and two from the Greek). The first eight are all baptismal: creation, Abraham's obedience, the exodus, God's love for Israel, a new covenant, life in God, clean water and a new heart, and baptism into Christ (Romans 6). With this the baptismal teaching ends, and the celebration of the resurrection begins with "Alleluia," the Easter gospel (Matthew 28, Mark 16 or Luke 24) and the eucharist that seals the whole long-term process of Christian initiation. (On the eucharist as "seal" of Christian initiation, see my book, *Confirmation:*

Origins and Reform, New York: Pueblo, 1987). No trivialization here; the tradition implies formal *public teaching.*

Conclusion

I say all this to show that what might be called the "liturgical *grammar*" of the presentations links them intimately to other elements, namely, the lenten and Vigil readings, and that the linkage is *public teaching of catechumens in the solemn presence of the church locally realized.* If this is true, it gives us the certain perspective within which to recommend certain specifics in performing the presentations themselves.

First, one should not read the rite's directions for the presentations as emphasizing merely the giving out of "ancient documents." These documents are essentially triggers for catechesis. They teach the assembled church *and* its catechumens the faith as this takes the forms of baptismal confession (the creed) and of prayer to God for salvation both now and in the eschatological future (the Lord's Prayer). Both these faith-forms are cardinal in every Christian's life: Without them neither baptism nor eucharist makes sense, for if we do not believe what we confess and pray, then all collapses into a rubble of infidelity, urges, programs, fads, ideologies and confusion. We become something less than a Rotary Club with hymns. This counsels us not merely to hand out texts but to *teach* them.

Second, perform the presentation on Sunday when the faithful are publicly gathered, not on a weekday when the faithful are largely absent. Any Sunday in Lent (during the time of election) will do, but scrutiny Sundays are preferable by far. The homily should constitute the *teaching* of the creed or Lord's Prayer, after which the actual document might be given to each of the catechumens, and the rest of the scrutiny liturgy—with its prayers, exorcism and dismissal of the elect—would conclude the service of the word. Such a procedure would focus two of the scrutinies on teaching basic faith in public. This is something of sufficient importance as to constitute an adequate reason for bending the rubrics in this instance.

Third, the local church would be eminently well served if this procedure is closely related to a consistent and well-executed policy of preaching throughout Lent from a baptismal perspective. The lenten season and its readings are an immeasurably rich source for such a well-worked-out homiletical program.

41

Fourth, catechists should see to it that their catechumens learn the creed and Lord's Prayer (in whatever form the two are used in the local church) by heart so that they can recite them out loud at the presentations. The catechumens' ability to do this is one point upon which it is reasonable for the assembly to scrutinize them in public. Although the most important thing is, of course, that catechumens understand creed and prayer, their ability to recite both from memory is not to be dismissed as mere rote learning. Both texts are liturgical parts which belong by right to the baptized in their public worship. One often sees people at Sunday Mass who stand mute as creed and prayer are recited. This suggests an indifference that is inappropriate to a faithful people, especially as they stand before God in Christ at the supreme act of Christian public worship.

5

Coming To Know
Jesus the Christ:
The First Scrutiny

Robert D. Duggan

Not long ago, I was contacted by a distraught director of the catechumenate in a nearby parish. It seemed the parish priest was refus-
ing to celebrate the scrutinies because he insisted that they were
inappropriate in our American cultural setting. They were, he insisted, exorcisms devised for primitive societies that still believe in
magic and occult possession. Sadly, this view, and the misunder-
standings it reveals, are all too often found even among those com-
mitted to the implementation of the RCIA. A better appreciation of
the nature of the scrutinies and the role they play in the journey of
the catechumens can serve to overcome such resistance.

Larger Context
The liturgical scholars who worked on the development of the RCIA
following the Vatican Council devoted careful thought and extensive
pastoral experimentation to the scrutinies and their part in the catechumens' overall conversion process. The scrutinies and the exorcistic prayer which they contain must be understood as part of that
final stage of the journey which begins at the celebration of the rite

---

Robert D. Duggan, pastor of St. Rose of Lima Parish, is on the Steering Committee of
the North American Forum on the Catechumenate. He edited *Conversion and the Catechumenate* and coauthored the *Catholic Faith Inventory.*

of election. Election and the time of purification and enlightenment that it begins are the context for all that happens in the celebration of the scrutinies. This is a special, sacred time in which there is a heightened sense of expectation and openness to the spiritual realities involved in the great drama of redemption. The lenten retreat that is punctuated on three successive Sundays by these powerful prayers for deliverance and healing provides the supportive framework and focus for understanding the meaning of the scrutinies. As the elect approach the final days of their journey to full initiation, the church pours out her most powerful prayers for God's grace.

In addition to looking at the larger context of the entire catechumenal journey and the setting of the scrutinies in the period of purification and enlightenment, one must interpret each scrutiny in its immediate context of the Third, Fourth or Fifth Sunday of Lent. There is, in fact, a progression that those who developed these rites had in mind as the prayers and rituals were elaborated. In the experimental version of these rites tested around the world in 1966–68, and in subsequent revisions made on the basis of those experiences, the scholars who worked on the rites came to describe a progressive spiritual movement that the scrutinies were meant to foster. Although a description of this thematic development never found its way into the final published texts, it is helpful to understand how that progression was envisioned.

Several Dimensions

The first scrutiny, using the story of the Samaritan woman, was meant to highlight particularly the reality of sin in its *individual* dimension. The second scrutiny, by means of the story of the man born blind, focuses on *social* sin. Using the powerful images of religious leaders who are blinded to the Christ and play on the fear and indifference of the man's parents, the story evokes the tragic impact of a community turned away from the light of truth. The third scrutiny, by means of the Lazarus story, focuses on sin and evil in its most radical dimensions: the hopelessness of those whose sin is unto death and whose only hope is in the One who is the resurrection and the life.

It would be overstating the case to say that each of the scrutinies is only about one of these themes. Obviously, in any of the celebrations, all of the themes can be found in one way or the other.

But it is helpful to keep in mind the potential for a progressive movement via the thematic development from one Sunday to the next. Rather than a straight-line development, perhaps a better image is a development that spirals around these mysteries, reaching deeper levels at each successive celebration. The point is an important one, because there are some attempts today to restrict the meaning of the scrutinies to one or the other focus. Some, for example, try to say that the scrutinies are about social sin only, that this is the time when we *must* focus on the structural evils of a world that would threaten to engulf us all, elect and faithful alike. Others insist that we deal in the scrutinies only with the personal sins of the elect, and any effort to celebrate the scrutinies in ways that identify the assembly of the faithful with the prayer for deliverance is wrong. This, too, is an interpretation that remains excessively narrow and fails to allow for the richness present in each of the scrutinies.

We should keep in mind the various contexts within which the scrutinies are celebrated: the respective Sundays of the lenten retreat, the total lenten period of purification and enlightenment, the lifelong journey of faith of those preparing for initiation. There is another immediate context within which the scrutinies are situated, and that is the liturgy of the word for the particular Sunday on which the celebration is to be held. We noted earlier that the developers of the RCIA used the gospel passages of the Samaritan woman, the blind man and Lazarus to guide them in their efforts to elaborate rites that celebrate a progressive confrontation with the mystery of sin. In his commentary on the third scrutiny, Mark Searle does an outstanding job of showing how the gospel narrative guides the meanings of the ritual actions. But we wish to insist here that *all* of the readings from a given Sunday must be part of the context out of which we interpret the meaning of any given celebration. As important as the gospel stories are for understanding the scrutiny ritual, we must not overlook the other readings which often point to meanings that are also important.

A final step in interpreting the scrutinies is confronting the symbol language of the rite itself. In this we must include the choreography of the ritual—the gestures and movements of participants, sounds and silences—as well as the prayers themselves, their images and allusions.

Particular Situation

When we have explored all that we have alluded to, we should have some sense for what scrutinies in general and a given rite in particular are all about. There remains at that point one last step, namely to factor into our understanding the uniqueness of a particular group of the elect and the particular community with whom we celebrate the rite. These situational factors are often as decisive for the meaning of a ritual as any of the "givens" which we might explore beforehand. For example, the tragic death of one of the elect may rivet an assembly's attention on some particular manifestation of the power of evil in their midst, and the meaning of the celebration of the scrutinies will be shaped by that awareness. Or the life of one of the elect may be a story of personal triumph over sin in some dramatic way known to all, and will cast a new light on the community's prayer for deliverance and healing. Such elements must also be carefully considered by those who prepare the ritual and reflect on its meaning.

Rite of Passage

The first scrutiny is the first rite that the elect celebrate following their election. Experience has shown the powerful, transforming effects that are felt by those who have undergone election. They have truly experienced a *rite of passage* that has given them a new seriousness, a deeper sense of purpose and direction. Something special is happening to them, they sense, and the bishop's solemn declarations at the cathedral have impressed on them the significance of the intensive period of prayer to which they have been called. The lenten liturgies have unfolded the themes of conversion, call to penance and struggle with evil, and they are experiencing a community that walks with them in penitential solidarity.

In the pastoral care of their catechumenal team, the elect should be called to reflect, perhaps with a spiritual director, on the reality of their lives if they are going to give over those lives completely to Christ. As the day of the first scrutiny arrives, they gather with the rest of the assembly to be nourished on the word.

Readings

The first reading from Exodus 17 offers the striking image of water flowing from a desert rock. But it also inserts into that scene a

46

community's grumbling against the Lord because of the hardships which have befallen them. For the elect experiencing perhaps for the first time the rigors of lenten penance, the text may have surprising connections. At any rate, it establishes a context in which the social sin of a grumbling community is met with divine grace—water in the desert—that quenches not only their thirst for water but also their doubts. ("Is the Lord in our midst or not?")

Psalm 95 is a joyous hymn to the rock of salvation. But the sobering admonition of its antiphon ("harden not your hearts") serves to maintain the serious mood established in the first reading. "They tested me though they had seen my works" is the sort of plaintive cry one could expect of a God against whom we have sinned. God inspires true contrition. We recognize in the ancient words of the psalmist the reality of our own sinfulness.

Romans 5 is a text that captures the experience of the elect as they approach initiation: Justified by faith, they have gained access to the grace in which they presently stand. What lies ahead is the "proof" of God's love, the dying of Jesus into which they are to be incorporated in a few short weeks. The love of God "poured out in our hearts" evokes subtle images of refreshing water—the water of love—that the gospel will spell out in story form. This text prepares us for the baptismal waters of the Vigil and the eschatological fullness of which every sacrament is a sign.

The narrative of John 4 dominates the liturgy of the word, not only by its length but even more by the sheer power of its images and message. This almost playful dialogue between Jesus and the woman at the well is one of the most polished Johannine stories. The universal journey of faith is compressed into the space of moments, as the woman challenges, probes, questions and finally yields to the presence of the Holy One. That which she thought she knew and that which she sought have been turned upside down and inside out. Her radical conversion is portrayed in terms that invite the hearer into a similar process. Conversion, in this perspective, is coming to know and accept Jesus the Christ—personally, deeply, totally. Intended or not, the movement of the readings has led directly to the Christ, precisely to the point from which every scrutiny must draw its power. It is now up to the homilist to make the connections between the scriptural proclamation, the journey of the elect, the life situations of this particular community and the ritual that is about to take place. In terms of what was said earlier about making the ritual *meaningful* to the assembly, it would be hard to overestimate how crucial the homilist's role is here.

One step in interpreting the meaning of the scrutiny is learning to read the symbol language of the rite which includes both the choreography of the word, gestures and prayers. We look now to the flow of the rite, its structure and its major symbolic components.

After the homily, the elect and their godparents come forward and stand before the presider as he addresses first the assembly and then the elect. The rite does not prescribe any specific text for these admonitions, nor does it provide a sample of the kind of message to be used, although it does give an indication of what is to be said. Both groups, the elect and the assembly, are urged to pray for a "spirit of repentance, a sense of sin and the true freedom of the children of God." Obviously, the presider's words here will be important in orienting all to the attitude of prayer that is appropriate. The elect alone are then directed to take a penitential posture by bowing their heads or kneeling.

Prayers

The body language that is involved in the scrutinies is important in the power of the rite. During the experimental period in the development of the RCIA, there was considerable revision in the body language used. Pastoral use in this country has generally indicated the advantage of asking the elect to kneel at this point rather than merely bowing their heads. Some communities adapt the ritual by asking the assembly also to kneel as a way of identifying itself with the elect in need of the church's prayer. While this option has certain elements to recommend it, by having everyone kneel the rite loses some of its expressive power by implying that the church is praying not merely *with* but *for* the elect.

The rite directs all to spend some time in silent prayer. It would seem that if the liturgy of the word has been full and rich, a very ample period of quiet prayer must be provided here. It would seem important to help stretch our communities' ability to spend time in quiet prayer together. Done properly, nothing is quite as powerful as an intense period of silence filled with prayer. Profound silence in a room filled with hundreds of people is as tangible an experience of the sacred as our liturgical tradition affords.

After the period of silent prayer, the elect are invited to stand with the assembly for the intercessions. Here again, pastoral experience in this country has indicated the value of adapting the body language by having the elect remain kneeling during the intercessions. The effect is to heighten the sense of a community praying over its brothers and sisters. The godparents are also told to place their right hand on the shoulder of the elect during the intercessions. Both of these elements emphasize the dependence of the elect on the prayer of the church during a time of radical vulnerability. Afterwards, the elect frequently give witness to the powerful experience of this ritual. They feel special bonds of love for those whose prayers have been lavished on them. It is not exaggerated to compare their reaction to patients' feelings for a doctor whose skill has helped to bring them through a dangerous illness.

After the intercessions are completed, the presider faces the elect for the prayer of exorcism. If the elect have been kneeling for the intercessions, it would seem best at this point to have them stand. The exorcism prayer has a twofold structure: a prayer to the Father during which the presider's hands are joined, and then a prayer to Christ during which the presider's hands are stretched out over the elect. Between the two parts of the prayer, an option is provided for laying hands "on each one of the elect."

Hands

The direction to keep one's hands folded during the prayer to the Father is quite puzzling. It is contrary to the customary position of palms uplifted, which is so familiar from our eucharistic practice. Consistency would suggest the same posture of solemn prayer as the Father is addressed during the first half of the exorcism. The ancient prayer of exorcism once used addressed the devil directly here, but contemporary framers of the rite wished to stress the church's prayer to the Father. That emphasis is best accomplished with hands extended and palms upraised, as we do in the Lord's Prayer when we ask to be delivered from evil.

The optional laying on of hands which comes next has proven to be one of the most powerful moments of the rite, provided it is done well. It is hard to imagine why one would omit this "optional" feature that speaks so eloquently of the caring, healing touch of Jesus mediated in the church. The hands are put directly on the head of the elect, not held over the head. And the touch is prolonged for some time while the presider prays silently for each individual in turn. This is again a time when silence seems preferable to "filler" music. Another pastoral adaptation of many communities is to have the godparents (and others) come forward to join in the laying on of hands. The silent procession of those who touch and pray for their brothers and sisters is a moving sign of the whole church at prayer, not just the presider. It is also a mechanism which creates the sort of bonding between persons that lasts a lifetime.

In the prayer to Jesus Christ which follows, the presider is directed to stretch out his hands over the elect with palms downward in the epicletic gesture familiar from the eucharist. The association of this gesture with prayer that invokes the coming of the Holy Spirit adds a trinitarian dimension which is subtle yet strong. As was the case with the laying on of hands, here too an invitation to the assembly to stretch out their hands with the presider during the prayer is a strong statement of the whole church at prayer. The Spirit is not given to the church by the presider; the Spirit is given by Christ and dwells in the church assembled at prayer. The presider's outstretched hands are visible signs of the assembly's mediation of that gift, and it makes great sense for them to join in his gesture.

Following the prayer of exorcism, a song may be sung. If what has just transpired has been as powerfully felt as it should be, then it seems almost imperative for a community to break into song at this point. Choice of music will have to be attentive to mood as well as text in order to capture the moment effectively here. Sentiments of praise, thanksgiving and joy are appropriate, but the atmosphere of seriousness that has pervaded the ritual should not be broken. Afterwards, the elect are dismissed and the celebration continues.

Conclusion

In the first part of this chapter, we discussed a number of issues that must be addressed as we comment on the rite of scrutiny and try to understand its meaning. We saw the need to place the rite in the various contexts that shape its meaning—the candidates' journey, the period of purification and enlightenment, the rhythm of the lenten Sundays, the scriptural proclamation, the symbol language of the rite itself. In brief form we have touched on several of these, hoping to model an approach that can be used in other rites as well. Mark Searle's article on the third scrutiny is cited for its careful attention to the context set by the gospel story of Lazarus. In this commentary on the first scrutiny we have attempted to pay particular attention to some of the elements of ritual choreography that can be so expressive and even determinative of the rite's meaning. In another chapter we will concentrate on the second scrutiny and in particular how the content of the prayers must be listened to carefully in order to understand the meaning of the rite.

God Towers over Evil: The Second Scrutiny

Robert D. Duggan

A "commentary" on a liturgical rite is a challenging task. There is, first of all, the need to understand the basic structure of the rite. Sometimes historical information about the development of the rite can be helpful here; other times, a simple analysis of the ritual as it stands is the best course. One must examine and try to understand the symbols of the ritual, from the objects used to the actions of the participants. There are also the contexts in which the rite is situated—its place in the liturgical cycle and the overall sacramental system, as well as the more specific contexts of particular celebrations. Finally, there are the texts themselves that are used and that must be looked at for the clues they give to the meaning of the rite.

In our comments on the first scrutiny, we stressed the importance of understanding how the contexts of the rite influence its meaning, and we spent considerable time examining the choreography of the ritual action. Mark Searle, in his commentary on the third scrutiny, looks closely at the roles and narrative structures of the ritual, especially in light of the gospel narrative of Lazarus read on the Fifth Sunday of Lent. In our remarks here on the second scrutiny, we

Robert D. Duggan, pastor of St. Rose of Lima Parish, is on the Steering Committee of the North American Forum on the Catechumenate. He edited *Conversion and the Catechumenate* and coauthored the *Catholic Faith Inventory*.

wish to show how important it is to attend carefully to the content of the prayers themselves in order to understand clearly the meaning of the rite.

We need to call to mind that the second scrutiny takes place on the Fourth Sunday of Lent, using Cycle A texts from the lectionary. Those scriptures are the anointing of David by Samuel (1 Samuel 16:1, 6–7, 10–13), the Shepherd Psalm (Psalm 23:1–6), the exhortation from Ephesians to live as children of the light (Ephesians 5:8–14) and the story of the man born blind (John 9:1–41). The sacramentary contains presidential prayers which pray in a specific way for those preparing for baptism. Those texts are distinctive for the theme of joy that runs through them, no doubt an echo of the "rejoice" motif from the day's entrance verse which gave this Sunday the popular name, *Laetare* ("rejoice"). We will not comment at length on any of these texts here other than to note that it is the gospel that provides the dominant scriptural imagery picked up as the "theme" of this week's scrutiny.

The story of the man born blind is a powerful symbol of what we today describe as "social sin." This blind man is an eloquent personification of the human experience of being caught in an evil not of one's own making. What medieval theologians would later develop in abstract terms using the notion of "original sin" finds in this primordial biblical symbol a forceful expression. Evil is always prior to us; it is the condition into which we are born. The blind man finds himself surrounded by Jewish leaders who conspire against anyone who would recognize Jesus as God's instrument of salvation; even his parents are caught up in the "conspiracy of silence" out of fear of the religious leaders of their time. The helplessness of the man in the face of this evil—his sense of being "caught" irrevocably—was the weight carried by this truly tragic figure. It is only with God's help (in Jesus) that a way out is possible. The passivity of the human condition is so much to the fore in the imagery of the man born blind, that God's initiative for salvation is inevitably thrown into sharp relief. The scriptural story tells us something about the scrutiny: Exorcism is an act of God (in the church). The elect are recipients of a gift, and their powerlessness over evil beyond their own making only serves to highlight exorcistic prayer as a work of grace.

The first of the texts provided in the ritual is the intercessions for the elect. There are two formularies given, with the note that both the introductions and the intentions may be adapted to fit various circumstances. Pastoral use in this country has discovered the tremendous advantages of drawing those intentions from a process of discernment with the elect, so that the community prays for deliverance from evils that are very real to the elect themselves. The process of having the elect name the demonic forces that afflict them serves as a model for the whole community which must also allow the lenten period to be a time of recognizing their own evils. Despite our encouragement of this practice of writing intercessions at the local level, it seems important to study carefully the models provided in the rite. The examples given there have much to say that can help us understand the nature of this prayer.

The first four intentions in example A deal directly with the elect; the remaining four with their families, the community and the needs of the whole world. (In example B, the ratio is six to two.) This gives us an important reminder that scrutinies, like every sacrament, are for the sake of the church and not just for one person.

The "world" of evil that we address in exorcistic prayer is larger than the petty list of sins one might sometimes find in a routine examination of conscience for an individual. We are about the work of cosmic redemption here! A list of intentions that neglected to name the larger evils of the world and concentrated only on the moral peccadilloes of the elect would be sadly impoverished. Example A contains frequent mention of the idea of freedom or liberation, another clue to the meaning of the scrutiny. Those who experience themselves bound and held captive are keenly aware of their longing for freedom. For those who often do not even recognize their bondage to sin, such prayer can heighten awareness and be the beginning of a movement toward conversion. This language is also part of another pattern that is marked in the scrutinies in general: the rhetoric of battle, opposition, struggle. There is frequent use of language that describes the experience of the elect as one of combat.

The point, it seems, is to say something about the nature of their journey as one in which good and evil are pitted against one another in mortal conflict. The struggle is one in which they face powers beyond their strength. We pray for their resistance, their perseverance and ultimately for their deliverance at God's hand. Yet, the somber realization that affliction, suffering and the cross are an inevitable part of the elect's journey is quite clear. How completely this perspective dominates the horizon of the intercessions is evident if we note that no explicit mention is made of the impending baptism, now only a matter of weeks away. The imagery is almost entirely that of the lenten combat.

Example B, in contrast to example A, also contains language that echoes the themes of darkness and light found in the gospel. Here again we see a use of language that plays upon opposites and polarity to show how incompatible are the forces of sin and grace. The language of this second set of intercessions seems much more evocative and poetic, and certainly better suited to a ritual use in which the texts are likely to be sung in solemn fashion.

After the intercessions, the rite continues with the prayers of exorcism. Two choices are offered, and we shall take a close look at both. The structure of the prayers is standard: an opening invocation of the Father, who is addressed with a specific title and then asked for a particular grace; a silent invocation of the Spirit by the laying on of hands; a closing invocation of Christ from whom appropriate gifts are sought, especially the gift of the Spirit.

The first prayer begins by calling upon the Father of mercy and then indicates the basis for that title: the gift of faith which led the man born blind to the kingdom. This faith has a specific quality about it; it is faith in God's Son. Likewise the kingdom is a particular one: the kingdom of light. In the space of just a few words, the prayer evokes some of the richest themes in all of the scriptures: faith, Son, light, kingdom. These are among the most evocative symbols in the Christian repertory of belonging, mystical vision and intimate personal knowledge of salvation.

There follow three requests on behalf of the elect: that they be freed from false values that blind them, that they be established in God's truth and that they be made children of the light. The expressions are poetic enough to allow a rather broad application, and they connect nicely with the imagery of the day's gospel. There is a subtle yet significant point made through this reference to the blindness of the elect. They stand not only with the man born blind who was victim of the evils around him ("the false values that surround"), but they—like the Pharisees in the gospel—must admit to a degree of complicity in the evils of the world. In asking that the elect be made children of light, an eschatological note is sounded, one that suggests the approach to the baptismal experience which will make of them the "enlightened ones," as the newly baptized were called in the ancient church. The language leaves little doubt that the effect brought about in the elect through God's action is a decisive ("forever") victory over all of the negative forces previously mentioned.

After the community's "Amen" and the laying on of hands, the presider continues with a prayer addressed to Christ the true light that enlightens the world, an obvious reference to the prologue of John's gospel. The request that is made of Christ is for freedom, an echo of the repeated request of the intercessions and a familiar theme throughout the scrutinies. There is a contrast established between the "Spirit of truth" who frees and the "father of lies" who enslaves. Such language of mutual opposition contributes mightily to the emotive tonality of the prayer and helps to sustain the martial context which is so consistent a feature of these prayers. The next request, "stir up the desire for good," seems somewhat bland in comparison, although the mention of "desire" in the same breath as "chosen for your sacraments" does capture the elect's longing for the approaching Easter sacraments.

In the final lines of the prayer, Christ is asked to allow them to "rejoice in your light" and make them "staunch and fearless witnesses." The first of these requests heightens our sense of the proximity to Easter joy, while the second emphasizes the consequences of the Easter mysteries. Particularly significant here is the glimpse we are given of what will become a constant refrain during the season of mystagogia: that transformation in Christ makes one a fearless witness to the faith. This is what happened to the man born blind, and this is what we ask for the elect. The apostolic dimension of the conversion experience is an essential one, and here it creates a horizon that extends beyond the candidates' sacramental initiation and into the rest of their lives. One thinks of the *boldness* described in the Acts of the Apostles as characteristic of the newly baptized and proof of the Spirit's power.

What we are seeing in these lines is a frequent phenomenon in liturgical prayer: The closer we approach to a major feast, the more our ritual language begins to anticipate the mood of what is coming. Consistent with this, we have seen in the texts of the first two scrutinies a very gradual lifting of our vision from the grim aspects of the lenten struggle to the joyous mood of Easter victory. In this prayer, for example, there are only fleeting references to the shadow of evil, while the majority of references are filled with positive imagery. Similarly, the prayers of the third scrutiny are filled with emphases on resurrection and new life.

Our careful look at the first of the options for the exorcism prayers in this scrutiny will make easier a review of the second option. Many of the characteristic features that we noted in the first prayer are true of the second as well and do not require extended comment. The prayer begins with an address to God as the "source of unfailing light." Throughout this prayer, there is frequent and consistent use made of the light and darkness imagery from the gospel, and this opening establishes the foundation for all that follows. Once again, a nice contrast is given between the "darkness of hatred and lies" and the "light of truth and love" that God pours forth upon the whole human family by the death and resurrection of Christ. As in the earlier prayer, the imagery is primarily positive, although there certainly is an acknowledgment of the strength of evil against which we pray.

In the first request of the prayer, the focus is on the elect and their impending baptism that will, as in the earlier prayer, "make them children of the light." We also ask that they may be made "adopted children," "delivered from the prince of darkness." Once again, we note the martial imagery as well as the anticipation of Easter's baptismal motifs. The content of this first prayer to God is perhaps not as rich as its counterpart in the earlier option, but there are nonetheless strong features that make it a credible option.

After the community's "Amen" and the laying on of hands, the presider's address to Christ is concise yet filled with rich imagery. The descent of the Spirit at the Jordan is linked to the empowerment of Jesus to proclaim the good news according to the servant prophecy of Isaiah 61. In the next sentence, where we ask the Lord Jesus to pour out "the same holy Spirit on these elect," we naturally expect a request to empower them for a similar mission of service. Disappointingly, the prayer does not follow the imagery through, but instead it asks that they be "guided," "kept safe" and come to see the Lord "face to face." While these are certainly valid concerns for us to petition the Lord about, it seems as if a valuable opportunity has been lost to show the consequences of baptism in terms of our mission of charity and justice. The role that Christ has in overcoming our blindness is much more than lifting individuals out of their private darkness; it is about making new Christians who will bring Christ's light to those who are in darkness because of a world where evil continues to afflict the little ones.

We have taken a close look in this article at the content of the prayers used in the second scrutiny. The rite itself is much richer than the content of the prayers alone, of course. We have already indicated that a full exploration of the meaning of any scrutiny would require more extensive analysis of other features as well. But we hope to have shown that one of the foundational elements in any attempt to understand the meaning of these rites is a grasp of what is said in the texts we pray.

We have discovered in these prayers a wealth of insight into the drama of sin and grace, human freedom and the slavery that is sin. We have seen the christocentric universe of the church at prayer; a universe that is trinitarian, to be sure, but one in which Jesus the Christ stands for us all as the one who forever delivers us from the powers of evil, no matter what form they may take. We have seen, likewise, something of the church's role in effecting that deliverance. Through the intercessory prayer of the church, the demonic in all its manifestations is conquered. Exorcism is a prayer that is efficacious because it is the prayer of the church, a prayer uttered in faith. This is the light we have been given that takes away all blindness: to see that Jesus Christ is Lord.

7

For the Glory of God: The Third Scrutiny

Mark Searle

One of the characteristics of authentic conversion is the tendency for converts to engage in what might be called "biographical reconstruction": the reinterpretation of their past lives in terms of the present. The classic instance is St. Augustine. In his *Confessions*, he tells the story of his life from the perspective of his conversion, remembering it not merely as a series of events and experiences but as a history of sin and deliverance. He finds not only his true self but also the God of his life: "If I find you apart from memory, I am unmindful of you. How then shall I find you, if I do not remember you?"

The period of purification and enlightenment, similarly, is a time set aside for the elect to recollect the stories of their past from the vantage point of their election, to discover in scattered and elusive memories the chiaroscuro of sin and grace and the slender thread of continuity by which they have been drawn by God, unwittingly and sometimes unwillingly, to the grace of this present moment. For this, the converts will need to draw upon the memories of the church, her stories, her symbols, her vocabulary. They provide the language and the framework for this task of "biographical reconstruction."

Mark Searle is associate professor of theology at the University of Notre Dame, coordinator of the Graduate Program in Liturgical Studies and associate director for liturgy in the Notre Dame Study of Catholic Parish Life. His publications include *Christening: The Making of Christians*, *Liturgy Made Simple* and many articles.

It is above all in the lenten scrutinies that what John Dunne has called "the search for God in time and memory" is undertaken. Here the church helps the elect reconstruct the story of their deliverance by presenting them with three narratives of deliverance: the man born blind, the Samaritan woman and the raising of Lazarus. As we shall see, these stories are proclaimed as paradigms for the elect, stories which enlighten their own experiences: What happened to these people in their encounter with Jesus is what is happening to you in your encounter with the risen Christ. To explore how the scrutinies work, we shall take just one example: the Fifth Sunday of Lent, the raising of Lazarus.

The Structure of the Scrutinies

To grasp the significance of the scrutiny on this Sunday it is useful to note who is involved and what is done and where.

At the center of the action are the elect. They have already accomplished a more or less lengthy journey of conversion and undergone a transformation of outlook and behavior. They are no longer the people they once were. They have become Christians and have been found ready for baptism, ready to assume a new identity before God in the body of Christ and to be solemnly incorporated into the common life of the faithful in the Holy Spirit. By the working of the same Spirit of Christ, they have been drawn away from their old ways of thinking and acting to serve the living God. Now, in Lent, they are consolidating that transformation and reconsidering the story of their lives. The story of Lazarus is the story of his encounter with Christ and his experience of the power of God to give life to the dead. For the elect, this ancient story is about to be reenacted: They are to see themselves in Lazarus and to find Christ summoning them to life through the mediation of his body, which is the church. This body is the congregation which surrounds them, whose unity is symbolized in the presence of the pastor who, in presiding, symbolically represents Christ, the head of the body. In the scriptures, in the congregation and in the presider, the elect confront the presence of Christ in different forms, the presence of the One who has power over life and death. In so doing, they—and we with them—hope to come to a deeper appreciation of the mystery of life, death and resurrection as it is at work in our own lives.

So the community assembles and listens to the voice of Christ in the scriptures, "since it is he himself who speaks when the holy scriptures are read in the church" *(Sacrosanctum Concilium, 7)*. In response to this word, interpreted in the homily, the church prays over those preparing for baptism. The elect come forward, accompanied by their sponsors, and stand before the presider. By assuming this new place before the assembly, they become the focus of the church's prayer and attention. The presider asks the community to pray for the elect that they receive "a spirit of repentance, a sense of sin and the true freedom of the children of God."

In nontheological terms this corresponds to the capacity for "biographical reconstruction" mentioned earlier, for the sense of sin, a spirit of repentance and a feeling of God-given freedom come only in the process of reinterpreting one's past. For sin is only recognizable as such in the light of grace, and the voice of God calling us to life and to freedom can be heard only by those who, in hearing that voice, see their situation as one of death and unfreedom. Salvation is possible only for those who know their need to be saved, but recognizing the need for salvation is already its beginning. Hence the need to reconstruct one's biography, to recognize in what often looks to have been a rather ordinary and unremarkable life the patterns of ignorance, enslavement and death. This is the spirit of repentance.

The elect are invited to put themselves in that position: to bow their heads in shame, to kneel "as a sign of their inner spirit of repentance" (RCIA, #152). Note that this is not a matter of burdening the elect with guilt: Precisely because the knowledge of their enslavement to sin comes in the very moment of their being freed and forgiven, their acknowledgment of guilt can be an occasion of great joy. But, whatever their feelings, the ritual act of self-abasement conveys an attitude of repentance and of hope, as the elect entrust themselves to the ministry of the church and the power of Christ.

After a period of silent prayer, during which the realities of the situation have had time to sink in, all stand and the community begins to intercede for the elect. Then, in the name of the whole church of God, the presider prays the solemn prayers of exorcism, addressing God and Christ. The first prayer is offered with joined hands. Between the prayers, the presider lays hands on each of the elect in silence. The prayer to Christ is offered with hands outstretched over the elect.

This rather unusual way of proceeding reflects the christology of the Johannine gospels read at the scrutinies. According to John, salvation comes from God the Father. Jesus, in turn, is the one sent by the Father, the mediator through whom the invisible God is seen and heard and known. Thus the double prayer reflects the distinctiveness of the roles of Father and Son and serves as an implicit reminder to the elect that they are assuming a new way of being: living before God in Christ in the church. It is regrettable that the texts of the rites do not allude more clearly to the role of the Spirit of God in this process.

Like Jesus in the gospel reading (John 11:41), and in his name, the church calls upon God, the "Father of life and God not of the dead but of the living," to manifest his glory by delivering the elect from the power of death. With arms outstretched in a gesture of committing the elect to the mercy of Christ, the church asks him who summoned Lazarus to life to do the same for these disciples of his who are preparing for baptism. But behind these rather straightforward undertakings—reading the gospel story, offering prayers for the elect— important clues are given as to how the church understands the mystery of life and death and how that mystery is at work in the lives of the elect as they pursue their "journey of conversion."

First, the mystery is proclaimed in the scripture readings, especially in the gospel, and then it is celebrated in the rites and prayers of the scrutiny.

The Gospel

It is possible to take an ancient drama, recast it in contemporary terms and still tell the old story. *West Side Story* is a modern version of *Romeo and Juliet*. What gives the classics their timelessness is not the specific details of the original version, which can create a distance between us and them, but the structural similarities between their stories and the stories of our own lives.

Something similar is at work when we hear the gospel proclaimed. The world of first-century Palestine is irrevocably lost to us, but the gospel lives because the patterns of its narrative speak to the deeper patterns of our own lives. If the story of Lazarus, then, is to illuminate the situation of the elect, we need to get at the underlying structure of the narrative and at the dynamics that govern the various roles in the story.

64

NARRATIVE STRUCTURE. The very length of the telling of this gospel story conveys an essential ingredient in the tale: that Lazarus fell sick when Jesus was far away, that it took what seemed like a very long time for Jesus to get to Bethany. Jesus heightens the sense of his distance and absence by waiting another two days before setting out for the place of death where Lazarus was to be raised on the third day(!). The absence and distance of Jesus, then, are part of the meaning of the story.

The sense of distance and delay is artfully enhanced by the author through the introduction of several discussions that, while they hold up the action, nonetheless advance the reader's understanding of what is at stake. There is the discussion with the disciples, raising the fear of danger to Jesus himself if he crosses back into Judea, but serving ultimately to highlight the autonomy and authority of Jesus, who will confront death on his own terms and in his own time (verses 9–11). This discussion also brings up the issue of discipleship as implying a willingness to share in the death of Jesus (verse 16).

A further delay occurs as Jesus halts outside the village where he holds conversations with Martha and with Mary. Each of these women in turn, friends and disciples of "the Teacher," makes a profession of faith in Jesus. Martha does so verbally, confessing him to be "the Christ, the Son of God, the one who is coming into the world," while Mary confesses her faith by falling at his feet in a gesture of adoration. In both instances, though more explicitly in the case of Martha who has been told by Jesus "I am the resurrection and the life...," the confession of faith is linked to an acknowledgment of his lordship over death.

Then, at the tomb the asides of "the Jews," whose hostility to Jesus has earlier been noted, raise once again the question of just how extensive the power and authority of Jesus is. This discussion seems to rile Jesus (such is the meaning of "he was deeply moved"), for it reveals their lack of faith in him.

Finally, the climax is postponed one last time by Martha's protest, which serves to underline the extremity of the situation confronting Jesus' authority. Lazarus is not only dead, his body has begun to corrupt. This does not deter Jesus, for nothing is beyond God's power. On the contrary, the more hopeless the situation, the more God's authority ("glory") will be manifest.

At last, the climax. By turning away from the immediate scene to address God in prayer, Jesus makes it clear that his authority is not his own and that his power comes from the one who sent him. Consequently, what is about to transpire is a manifestation of the Father in the person, words and actions of the Son. Throughout the story, the initiative lies with the Father. It is God who, through Jesus, exercises an unlimited power to save, even from the awful finality of death. So Jesus commands the dead man to come out of his grave. The dead man hears his voice and obediently comes to life as the trappings of death are removed by disciples at Christ's command.

Many recognized the hand of God in this event and thus acknowledged God's glory in Jesus. Others, however, saw Jesus—not God— and hurried back to Jerusalem to set afoot that sequence of events that would encompass the death of him who summons the dead to life.

ROLES. As in any story, each role is a configuration of relationships and each actor is defined by the relationships that establish his or her place in the story.

Jesus is first identified in terms of his love for Lazarus and his sisters (verses 3 and 5). But he is far away, absent from them, across the Jordan with his disciples when Lazarus falls ill. He is there because of the hostility he has experienced in Judea. Indeed death has already cast its shadow over him: He has been washed and anointed by Mary, as if for burial; "the Jews" have tried to stone him; Judea is hostile territory. Yet he is also identified in the story as "Son of God" (verse 4) and at one with God (verses 22 and 42). Thus his actions are determined neither by his love for his friends nor by fear of his enemies, but solely by the commission he has from God, a commission that will manifest God's glory, that is, God's saving power at work in the world. God is manifested in Jesus as being able to summon both the living and the dead to life.

The *disciples* include both the household at Bethany and those who were with him across the Jordan ("our friend Lazarus," verse 11). Note that it is said of Lazarus, Mary and Martha, not that they loved Jesus, but that Jesus loved them. That is what enables them to bring their crisis to Jesus' attention. Later they address him as "Lord" and refer to him as "the teacher," thus revealing their discipleship. Of the other disciples, none are named except "the Twin." A "twin" is an exact copy, and it is "the Twin" who says, "Let us go also, that we might die with him," thus suggesting the role of the disciple as one who shares in the death of Christ.

There are, on the other hand, *the Jews* who represent the rest of the world, for the story relies on a basic opposition between believer/unbeliever, disciple/Jew, love/hostility. At the end, many, but not all, are converted and come to be disciples of Jesus. (Care must be taken to ensure that "the Jews" in the Fourth Gospel retain a representative function. The designation should not provide a basis for anti-Semitism.)

"Death" is also an actor, a role whose power grows as the story proceeds. Lazarus is ill, then dead, then prepared for burial, then buried, then corrupting. Death also threatens Jesus, as we mentioned. Yet it is precisely when death seems irrevocably triumphant—note the emphatic details of "tomb," "cave," "stone," "bandages," "cloth"— that its power is broken. But "death" is an ambivalent term. The story relies on the realization that physical death is a symbol of spiritual death, a form of death that is associated with the absence of Jesus and with images of darkness, stumbling, hostility, sleeping and unbelief. This is a form of death that may affect the living as well as the dead.

"Life" is likewise an ambivalent term. There is bodily life, the life lived before death, the life restored "at the resurrection at the last day." But this is merely "living and half-living" compared with the real life of which it is but a metaphor. This other life is the life of which Jesus speaks when he says, "he who believes in me, though he die, yet shall he live" (verse 25). This new life is associated with walking in daylight, in the light of Jesus, "the light of the world" (verse 9), and believing in him: "Whoever lives and believes in me shall never die" (verse 26). This life, which is the life of the risen Jesus and no mere resuscitation, is the gift of God to the living as well as the dead. It is offered now: "I am [present tense, in contrast to Martha's faith in a future bodily resurrection] the resurrection and the life" (verse 25).

The raising of Lazarus is a "sign," a manifestation of God's power to give us a share in his own eternal life for those who have the faith to acknowledge Jesus as Son of God and thus obey his voice. As St. Irenaeus put it: "The glory of God is [revealed in] the living person; but the life of a living person is the vision of God." This story, then, is not about revivification but about sharing the life of God by hearing the voice of Jesus. This summons to new life transcends the usually sharp dichotomy between death and mortal life, for God can reach even the dead: "Truly, truly, I say to you, the hour is coming, and now is, when the dead will hear the voice of the Son of God, and those who hear it will live" (John 5:25). None are so far gone that the voice of the Son of God cannot reach them and awaken them out of their deadly sleep. Such predicaments are "not unto death . . . [but] for the glory of God so that the Son of God may be glorified. . . ." (verse 4).

The Scrutiny

Finding themselves in this story, the elect are to find the presence and power of God in their lives: "How shall I find you if I do not remember you?" This involves, as we saw, a double discovery: the discovery that they have, in fact, been in some profound ways dead and that, at the same profound level, they are being commanded by Christ to "come forth."

This, in fact, is what the church believes to be the case. Hence the scrutiny, in which God and Christ are asked to do for the elect what they did for Lazarus. Look at what the prayers say about God, about Christ and about the past and the future of the elect.

ROLES. The prayers of the scrutiny are clearly addressed to the same God who is the active presence behind the story of Lazarus and whom Jesus addresses as "Father." The church, as body of Christ, also presumes to address God as "Father": "Father of life and God not of the dead but of the living." This God is "source of all life," who is manifest in giving life to the living and raising the dead. This same God sent the Son "to proclaim life, to snatch us from the realm of death and lead us to resurrection." In so doing, God demonstrates divine authority over death and reclaims human beings who will mirror God's glory.

Christ, in the scrutinies as in the gospel, is the one sent by the "Father" to proclaim the good news, to rescue us from the fate of final death and to bring humankind to a new, more abundant and immortal life. Prayer A, 2 (RCIA, 175) is the only one to suggest that Christ does so by giving the Spirit "who gives life." Prayer B, 2 expresses the conviction that this new life is already available to all humanity, not because Jesus brought Lazarus back to life but because he himself broke the bonds of death and was raised to a qualitatively new and different life in the resurrection.

The church prays for the elect that this gift of life may be theirs also. In so doing, she describes their condition in somber terms. They are under "the death-dealing power of the spirit of evil" (A, 1), "in the grasp of death" (A, 2), the prey of the "spirit of corruption." The alternative prayers make the same point, describing the elect as subject to "the tyranny of death" and "the slavery of Satan, the source of sin and death." Their situation is that of Lazarus. Like Lazarus, they may be "dead," yet they are able to hear the voice of Christ summoning them from the dead, for they are described as eagerly awaiting the "life-giving sacraments," as longing for new life through baptism, as eagerly approaching the waters of new birth and being hungry for the banquet of life.

Their present situation is ascribed to another actor: Satan. It is this "spirit of evil" that has them in its grasp. To this Satan is ascribed all sin and death and the corruption of a world that God created and saw to be good. Even though they have come to yearn for liberation, "the power of death" may still "hold them back" (B, 2).

That is why the church prays in the scrutinies for nothing less than what Jesus did in the last and greatest of his "signs" at Bethany in Judea. God is asked: "Free these elect. ..." "Free from the grasp of death those who await your life-giving sacraments and deliver them." "Rescue them. ... Free them. ... Place them under the reign of your beloved Son." This is to be done "through your Spirit, who gives life," and consists in their being filled with "faith, hope and charity."

IMPLICIT NARRATIVE. From this analysis of the roles being played out in the scrutiny, we can see that they approximate the roles identified in the gospel story. The same God, commissioning the same Christ to "snatch us from the realm of death," is beseeched again to raise these elect. The role of the church overlaps with several in the gospel: with Martha and Mary whose service of and friendship with the Lord occasions his intervention in the first place; with Martha and Mary especially in their faith in Jesus as "the Christ, the Son of God, the one who is coming into the world," a faith that allows Jesus to manifest the glory of God in their midst; with the disciples who move the stone and unbind the dead man at the Lord's command. Thus, as a company of disciples, the church has its work to do in assisting the Lord in his mission of raising the dead. But it is important to note, too, how the church presumes, by virtue of her identity as body of Christ, to speak to the Father in Christ's name, knowing she will be heard because of her unity with him. Thus, the efficacy of the church's prayer depends on her union with Christ, and the efficacy of her pastoral mission depends on her total subordination, with Christ, to the will of the Father.

As for the elect, their being commanded to come forth to new life depends in part on their being able to recognize themselves in the person of Lazarus and to accept the church's description of them as being enslaved to Satan and held in the tyranny of death. This is only possible through an act of "biographical reconstruction" in which they compare their past and their present. Here the gospel's emphasis on the absence and distance of Jesus and on the repeated delays that occurred before he arrived at the tomb may resonate with the elect's own experiences, as they review a lifetime lived, apparently with Christ over the horizon. What this means more precisely, and what "new life" means, is for each of them to discover during these days of purification and enlightenment.

In so doing, they will line their own life stories up with the narrative unfolding in the rite. These men and women have been held in the grasp of death and in the death-dealing power of the spirit of evil. Now, at the behest of the church, God is to intervene through Christ to set them free. They look forward to the life-giving sacraments of baptism and eucharist, but the church prays that they might already begin to experience the new freedom that God gives even as they wait. They are to be placed "under the reign of your beloved Son" (B, 1) even now, but certainly in baptism. Thus, by God's power, they are being drawn from death to life, from slavery to freedom, from life apart from Christ to life in Christ.

Henceforth they will adopt a new way of being in the world, one described as "life in the risen Christ" and "sharing in the power of Christ's resurrection." This life, lived in union with Christ in faith, hope and charity (A, 2), is not entirely theirs, for it is to be a life of witness: witness to the new life that is in them (A, 1) and thus witness to the glory of God before all humanity (B, 1). They will become signs, witnesses like Lazarus, of God's power over death, and thus revelations of the glory of God.

Conclusion

In this article we have taken the gospel reading and prayers for the scrutiny of the Fifth Sunday of Lent and pulled them apart to examine the roles and narrative structures underlying each. Even this has been done only partially, for the first two readings of this Sunday have been left aside, as have the intercessory prayers offered by the faithful on behalf of the elect. (We note that the first set of intercessions are generic in nature, owing little to the scripture readings of the day, while the alternative set hews closely to the gospel narrative and should properly have been included here, had space allowed.) Nonetheless, this should be enough to show what the scrutinies are for and how they work.

Celebrating
the
Solemn Vigil

Raymond B. Kemp

The novelty has worn off for those select few who choose to celebrate the Easter Vigil. Its popularity is on the low end of a scale that has Ash Wednesday and Palm Sunday on a high draw. "They'll come out in droves," said the first pastor, "if you give them something."

Argue with the assumption here, but let's be honest: Those of us most dedicated to the solemn celebration of the Vigil of Easter have not run out of tickets. There's room in most of our large churches for another couple hundred participants. The Easter Vigil is packed precisely when it is *not* a vigil but is a Mass of Easter Sunday.

That's just as well in parishes where the Vigil is the time for the parish to hear the word, baptize, confirm, celebrate eucharist with the newly baptized—and bring in Easter for those who are working with the Lent/Easter agenda of the church. Those parishes need the space. They do not need the encumbrance of crowds of watch checkers and homily timers.

But we who "work" the Triduum and the Vigil need to speak more clearly and more often about those parts of the Vigil we love, about what moves us and what stills us in the Vigil. Otherwise we

Raymond B. Kemp, pastor of Holy Comforter and St. Cyprian Church, Washington, DC, author of *Journey of Faith,* director of RENEW for the archdiocese of Washington, has lectured widely on RCIA.

leave the field to those who cut and paste a Vigil to try to fit the Saturday vigil Mass for a Sunday. And in doing so, we are threatened with losing the value of the reform and the significance of the catechumenate.

The question is clear enough: What do you like in the Vigil? What part of the Vigil moves or stills you, entices you into the saving mystery, intrigues you with further possibilities, invites you to prayer? Reread the question and slow down. Your answer will be different from that of the person with whom you share this article.

I think we need to approach our celebration of the Vigil asking what advantage participants can derive from the way we shape Easter Eve. Just as some of us have been enthralled with Trappist Matins at 4:30 AM and others have been lifted in the ordination of a special friend, we have to explore the pieces of the Vigil in a personal way before it will achieve its attractiveness for more and more of our parishioners.

I find it interesting that what means the most to me is contained in the presider's direct addresses to the assembly at the beginning of the Vigil, before the liturgy of the word, before baptism, the invitation to prayer before confirmation and the address to the assembly before their renewal of baptismal promises. Reread those interventions, especially if you are looking for some handles to grab onto the Vigil in a fresh way.

The opening invitation to come together in vigil and prayer, to honor the memory of the death and resurrection indicates a flavor for the evening that combines Irish wake and American testimonial meals. This is an evening of gathering first because we want to gather to pray and keep a vigil. You really should stay home if you do not want to gather with others to pray.

Keeping a vigil indicates darkness—gathering in the darkness to feel the warmth of being together in association with Christ and to transform the dark side of night (dying) with the new light of Christ. One of the reasons the Vigil flops is that our churches sit people down in rows and not around a table. The re-creation of our spaces for assembling people as a human community is never felt so keenly as in working this evening in space that prohibits gathering.

Outside and inside, in darkness and in light, the participants need to feel one another's presence, reach and touch one another, and know that they are not alone.

Being with the elect or with those who are to be received, confirmed and invited to eucharist for the first time is quite honestly the best part of the Vigil for me. Just as the ordination or profession of a friend can forgive a multitude of liturgical or personal gaffes, so the anticipation and excitement of those for whom we pray has to find a way to be communicated to those who gather even before they gather.

This happens when those who have come to know catechumens are many and varied and when catechumens and candidates reflect the variety of people in the parish: age, sex, cultural backgrounds, jobs, schooling and neighborhoods. If the catechumenate is central to the life of the parish and the parish knows the candidates, then this celebration is very personal.

But the other elements have to possess a simple attractiveness that has its own rewards. The liturgy of the word has to help people hear the stories of our tradition and bring them home. While gimmicks abound, sometimes a simple engaging of people in listening—quiet, reflective music, tasteful visuals—a true storytelling, campfire mood has been a rewarding respite.

If the only light is the Easter candle and the light for the reader, participants feel others listening. If there is a psalm that does not take a printed text to sing and a prayer time that is quiet for prayer instead of the awkward pause that finds all wondering "what's next?" then the liturgy of the word can be a good time for people.

If some slides of the community or the catechumens can be tastefully introduced here, if the community can see itself in preparation for this night, if visually the people become part of the story sharing, then these moments after the *Exsultet* and before the baptism can be a real exposition of the word.

Liturgical ministers need to convey by the way they carry themselves that this period of the liturgy of the word is important in itself. The selection of a fourth or fifth reading from the Hebrew Scriptures instead of the required three might signal our intention to take these stories seriously. Those in the sanctuary and taking principal roles *have* to say by their bearing: Relax and listen.

"The Creation Story" by James Eldon Johnson or the selection of music that might be culturally sensitive can serve to enliven this period, but the concern is that too many adaptations might be "cute" but not inspiring. Doing things well what is there will be a good beginning.

The homily has to bring us—all of us—into those stories. If the homily is worth its place tonight, it has to put us in the readings and the readings into this context first. Then the homily has to push us into the water. All of us are going into the water *and* pouring the water. The church is going to work tonight to generate and regenerate itself in dying and rising.

Remember the large garbage cans painted white and filled with water sitting in the sanctuary stage left? Remember when oil had to be poured into certain waters and the presider got it wrong? We have rescued ourselves from some of that, but the litany, the blessing and the baptisms are hardly lovable, attractive items in many a parish.

You have to scratch to find a church where water is more than a punch bowl and baptism is more than a sprinkling. If the water is flowing and doing its job, the assembly can get into a baptismal frame of mind. A litany over those who are prostrate before baptism or over those who are processing to a baptistry has to call the saints above into this space. The congregation does not have to see the baptisms in order to participate. We have to know the importance of water because we see it in our churches.

If you are doing water baptism in the cathedral parish of Yakima, Washington, or the co-cathedral of Honolulu, you know that the place of baptism is holy because there space is reserved for water to flow, and people have access to that water and to the presence of the Spirit in the water—they can visit the water—when they need to know the power of the bath.

In my current church, the permanent place for baptism is now the stand for the money box for the church goods store. Baptismal water flows out of a pitcher into a gallon-capacity stainless-steel salad bowl that deacons adjust to catch the trickle.

The only saving grace to this part of the rite is the face of the neophyte who is seen crying or smiling. How much better if they went off to be baptized while we sang and prayed in response to the invitation to help them by our prayers. Then we could greet them when they returned in their robes with their godparents as we sing acclamations with spontaneous (really spontaneous) applause.

I believe our parishes could have a vicarious water experience just by having seen the font, the water and the possibilities for immersion. And water for baptism needs to be carried now from the font to the people. Everyone has to get wet in the Easter bath.

Whether the baptismal area is in the church proper or apart, this bath can be part of their experience. And confirmation can be the whole church's confirmation of the baptism of these neophytes if we would invite people to pray over the neophytes by extending their hands and/or clustering around them. The peace here and in the eucharist should be tender moments.

Ah, the eucharist! So often an afterthought in a Vigil, something to finish quickly! Why not a break between the renewal of baptismal promises and the general intercessions? I mean a five-minute *break*. Organ or other instrumental interludes could be played, the sanctuary prepared, even the offering taken, bathrooms opened and then, on signal, the general intercessions are sung, followed by a simple preparation of the gifts and a full-bodied—standing—eucharistic prayer, with communion under both forms in abundance, of course, finally breaking the fast begun Holy Thursday night with one grand party for the neophytes and everyone in attendance. Start to finish: two to three hours depending on music, number of neophytes, cultural adaptations and seriousness of purpose. "But we're so bushed we can't get through Easter Sunday when all the people are there." Tell them what they missed like you mean it.

Happy Easter!

9

Sacraments of Initiation at the Easter Vigil

Richard N. Fragomeni

All is ready; the community has prayed, fasted and given alms for 40 days with the elect. The first two days of the Triduum are past, and the great night of Paschal Memory has arrived. The darkness of the springtime night is illuminated by the fullness of the moon, as the vigil fires of Easter burn. All is vibrant in the promise of the One whose dying and rising brings hope in the midst of human finitude and purpose to the work of our hands. The assembly is gathered, the stories are recounted and the metaphors of salvation once again enchant human ears, alluring us more deeply into a world that is our true home, the world of God's justice.

Before the night is consummated at the table of immortality, we do to others what has been done to us. Our ancestors have handed down through the centuries a prescription of a water bath, an oiled touch and a kiss. With these cosmic elements we invoke the spirit of the risen Christ to bind into the body a new harvest of apostolic witnesses. Washed in the blood of the lamb, these newly illumined join with us to dine at the center of the universe, the fountainhead of human history, regenerated as the new creation.

Richard N. Fragomeni, a priest of the diocese of Albany and former director of its Office for Liturgy, is currently completing doctoral studies in liturgy at the Catholic University of America.

The Paschal Vigil is the festival at the heart of the Christian year. Its celebration, in the context of the Triduum, has been given significant attention by liturgy planners for decades.[1] Moreover, in the RCIA, the Vigil receives added significance and calls for further planning and consideration by catechists and liturgists alike. The retrieval of the catechumenate as a functioning order within the church has made the Easter Vigil what it was and what it was always meant to be: a night of initiation and a cosmic festival of regenerated humanity.

This chapter examines the renewed rites of initiation as celebrated at the Paschal Vigil. Our concern here is to explore the rites of initiation for the elect—the unbaptized. We will not speak of the rites of reception into full communion nor of the combined rites for the elect and candidates for full communion that are currently part of the United States edition of the RCIA. These important discussions are the topics of other essays. This chapter will be a theological and pastoral overview of the initiatory rites that we celebrate during the night of Paschal Memory, as the climax of the catechumenal journey. It will be the task of these pages to look at the components of the initiation rituals within the context of the Easter Vigil, the mother of all vigils and the centerpiece of the Christian calendar.

A Theological Prelude
to the Easter Sacraments

The celebration of the sacraments of initiation at the Paschal Vigil are a part of the larger cycle of rites that punctuate the conversion journey of those who are called to share at the apostolic table of God's reign. Baptism, confirmation and eucharist are the tripartite climax that both end the catechumenal process of formation and inaugurate the lifelong mystagogy that is a hallmark of Christian life. The initiation of Christians is accomplished in stages, for the whole of Christian life is caught up in the ongoing transformation of consciousness and activity brought about by the power of the Spirit.

---

[1] For a synopsis of the rites of the Easter Vigil a good resource is Rupert Berger's work, *Celebrating the Easter Vigil* (New York: Pueblo). For a fine pastoral overview with liturgical suggestions see the annual *Sourcebook for Sundays and Seasons* (Chicago IL: Liturgy Training Publications). Also see Kenneth Stevenson's article about the paschal fire and its significance and placement, "The Ceremonies of Light: Their Shape and Function in the Paschal Vigil Liturgy," *Ephemerides Liturgicae* 99 (1985), 170–85.

This transformation bears fruit in communities of compassion at the broken centers of our history.

Such a perspective is not always operative among those whose care it is to order and direct the catechumenate and the paschal-night festivities. As often reported, the Easter Vigil has been treated as a "graduation" exercise at which the newly baptized are given all the "sacramental" rights and privileges of their newly earned status. This unfortunate treatment is played out not only at the Vigil (which, in some parishes, includes speeches after communion by the "valedictorian" or by a representative of his or her biological family, reporting how wonderful the catechumenate was—something akin to the evangelical testimonies of guests at the Crystal Cathedral) but also throughout the catechumenal journey itself, which is structured as an education program with the expectation that God's grace operates within the time of a school-year operation.

This programmed approach to the initiatory activity of the church insults the meaning of membership in the body of Christ by reducing initiation to a trivial pursuit of memorized facts and cozy feelings. The fact is that initiation is a birthing activity with the wailing and pain that accompanies all giving of life. For the paschal night to mean death and rebirth in Christ, those responsible for the formation of catechumens must attend to the signals of growth in each candidate and be ready to assist those on the journey of faith to interpret each moment of decision in full view of the gospel all along the route. Without a foundational commitment to works of justice that reach beyond the parochial limits into neighborhood and world, Christian initiation is incomplete. (We thus perpetuate the hoax of a bourgeois Christianity and the neat package plan of salvation that accompanies it.)

The Easter sacraments find their proximate context in the readings, prayers and gestures of the Easter Triduum. The images of lamb, Passover blood, bread, cup, water, washed feet, servant, high priest, cross, creation, Isaac bound, exodus, hope, promise, new hearts and empty tombs accompany the Christian assembly into the struggles of initiation into Christ, brought to crescendo during the paschal night.

It is often said that the sacraments of initiation are what give real meaning to the Easter Vigil, so that without them the Vigil makes little sense. This notion puts pressure on parishes to have catechumens ready each year. While I would agree with such a statement in

81

principle, it must be qualified by saying that the proclamation and testimony of the word are what most significantly proffer to the imagination of the Christian assembly the authentic meaning of initiation into Christ. The Vigil can proffer such meaning without the celebration of baptism and confirmation, albeit in an incomplete fashion.

Practically speaking, this means that liturgy planners and catechumenate ministers should not feel that they must "graduate" another class each Easter in order for the ritual to work. Sensitivity to the preparedness of those seeking initiation, not the exigencies of liturgical propriety, is the essence of discernment. It further means that we should give extreme care in the preparation of the readers for the Vigil and of the paschal homily, both in content and delivery.

What the Paschal Vigil celebrates is the core energy of the Christian tradition: dying and rising in the desires of compassion. The life of the Christian is caught up in savoring this mystery and reincarnating it in the world. In other words, Christians are mystagogues. Living within and from the mystery of the Champion of the Underworld, Jesus Christ, Christians seek justice and maneuver in the structures of power to transform them in hope. To ease the neophytes into such a life of living testimony, a life of mystagogical activity, the period of mystagogy proper functioned traditionally in a 50-day cycle but is now extended to a year cycle in the statutes of the United States. Unfortunately, in many places this is where the process of initiation fails.

We know that many of the newly baptized, after their "graduation," never return to "class." Like the adolescents whom we keep on the line for confirmation until their junior year of high school, we may never see many of them again. Many pastoral ministers involved in the catechumenate see this happening and find its cause in the lack of a vision of mission within the catechumenate period. Holistic catechesis calls for a focus on mission as integral to the formation of new Christians. This places a demand on the parish as a whole to adopt such a missionary vision. It is here that we may discover the greatest boundary of resistance. What is at issue here, then, is the ecclesial preunderstanding upon which the RCIA is built and which the great Fifty Days highlight by the readings from the Acts of the Apostles.

The paschal night is about the transformation of desires. It is the celebration of what continues to be done in the community by the indwelling of the Spirit who directs us to communicative action for the life of the world. The community rejoices in the memory that the Christ surrendered the most fundamental desire of survival into a death that transformed this desire to an alternative way of being: a way of consecrated becoming for others, a desire to be nourishment in the hope of compassion.

The Paschal Vigil is radiant with fire and stories, crowned with bread and wine, giving meaning to all who identify with Christ's mission.

Within the context of this theological prelude, we now examine the liturgical rhythm of the celebration of the sacraments of initiation at the Paschal Vigil.

A Pastoral Overview of the Rite

With the readings proclaimed, the candidates for baptism are presented to the assembly. The ritual book (#219) offers three options about how this can happen. The options hinge upon the placement of the font in relationship to the table and ambo. To accompany the movement to the font, wherever it is positioned, the Litany of the Saints is sung. The litany song-form is the traditional musical genre used in Eastern and Western liturgies to bring a procession alive and give meaning to the movement. In this case, at the Easter Vigil, we call to memory the lives of our ancestors who once were brought to such waters, finding in baptism the power of the death that overcomes death. In the singing of the litany, music ministers can add the names of other saints and petitions to the chant. Cantors can elaborate the names of the saints to make room for a more interesting musical line and a simple form of catechesis. For instance, instead of singing, "St. Stephen," the litany could enhance the memory of the ancestry by singing, "St. Stephen, first witness to the Risen One." The use of several cantors can enrich this musical accompaniment of preparation for baptism.

As the community stands around the font in the company of the saints, the water is now blessed (#222). Because David N. Power addresses this portion of the rite in detail, it is sufficient here to mention that the use of an acclamation by the people within the prayer makes this blessing come alive. A sample antiphon is printed on the next page. This type of antiphon can be used in the blessing prayer, punctuating it with the assembly's response. *(Liturgy, 6, #2).* Presiders

Gathering of the Waters

The "Blessing of the Waters" is the conclusion of a gathering service composed by David N. Power (text) and Richard N. Fragomeni (music). Two presiders and two cantors lead the service. During the singing of the antiphon after each blessing, water bearers bring the water from the congregation and pour it into a central font.

The Blessing

Presider One:

Gather them, my people, gather them from the four corners of the land.
Gather them from meadowland and mountain, from coastland and heartland, from rain-soaked plains and arid deserts.
Gather them from across mountains and rivers.
Gather them from beyond the seas and from beyond the confines of our storied land.
Gather them into one, to hear in a diversity of tongues but one speech of heart.
Gather them to be reborn in the life-giving waters.

Cantor I:

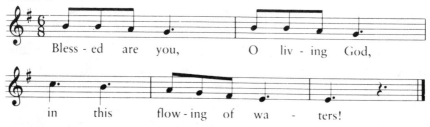

People's Response

Presider Two:

We shall now bless God in the gathering of the waters and in the gathering of the people. You are here from many regions and from beyond this land. As in your heart, you hear the text of the blessing and hear it call you, please rise to your feet. Those who have not risen by the final invocation will do so then, to join with all in proclaiming God and a new birth of church.

Presider One:

God, you delight my soul.
You pitched the tent, the sky, made rooms to store water, using clouds for a roadbed,

making the sea a blanket to cover the mountains.
Before your thundering voice, the waters raced away, running across hills, finding
  holes in every place.
The torrents tumble free, to water humans and cattle and wild animals.
From the heavens, the rains drop down to soak the earth, renewing all living things.
Blessed are you, God, in this flowing of waters.

[Cantor I and People's Response as before]

Presider Two:
With the mighty Mississippi and Missouri you have divided our land, watering it right
and left, giving it freshness and the source of life, filling those who dwell close to its
banks with the wonder of its might, causing them to tremble before the destruction
of its swell.
Blessed are you, God, in these waters, in their blessing and in their curse.

Cantor II:

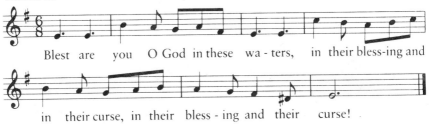

Blest are you O God in these wa-ters, in their bless-ing and
in their curse, in their bless-ing and their curse!

[People's Response as before]

Presider One:
Both blessed and accursed are your people in the waters of the Great River, the Rio
  Grande that both joins and separates people of different lands.
How wonderful the flow that invitingly welcomes the refugee across its span, how
  dread the return of the miserable to whence they came.
Blessed are those on desert plains when they draw refreshment from this great river,
  accursed are they when it runs dry and offers but a mirage of life.
How glorious its point of origin on mountain tops, how splendid its rivalry with the
  flow of the Colorado and its lakes.
Blessed are you, God, in these waters, in their blessing and in their curse.

[Cantor II and People's Response as before]

Presider Two:
O mighty force of the Atlantic that batters coasts from north to south, that eats into
  bays and estuaries, that fascinates and awes with its great swell.
Blessed are these waters that gave passage to the poor of foreign lands, that brought
  the tired and homeless to safe harbor.
Accursed the grave where it buried so many victims, so many hopes.
Blessed are you, God, in these waters, in their blessing and in their curse.

would do well to consider inviting the assembly to extend hands over the water as a gesture of blessing while the prayer is said or sung, depending on the gifts of the leader.

The readings, the homily, the litany of the saints and the water blessing prayer lead the community into a world of meaning: The Paschal Memory of Christ. It is into that world that the elect are about to be baptized. Because the anointing with the oil of catechumens has been suppressed at this point by the revised ritual, the renunciation of sin and the profession of faith become the immediate entry point into the water. Robert Hovda deals with this ritual movement in the chapter on the renunciation of evil and profession of faith. For now it is enough to say that the questions must be asked clearly so that they become public faith proclamations of these candidates as they enter with the community into the mystery of Christ.

The next action is the water bath itself. This is accomplished either by immersion, the first and preferred option, or by infusion (#226). In either case, the water should be plentiful and the words that accompany the action can be sung or proclaimed robustly with a sung acclamation by the assembly to conclude the action. A tune for the baptismal formula, composed by this author, is included as an example of what can by sung at this juncture after the candidate is addressed clearly by name.

I bap - tize you, in the Name of the Fa-ther, and of the Son and of the Holy Spi - rit.

The assembly is invited to respond by singing an acclamation such as an Easter Alleluia or one found in *Worship,* especially "You have put on Christ," (#112) by Howard Hughes, SM.

No parish fonts throughout North America were constructed for full body immersions. Nevertheless, creative parishes wishing to keep the symbol of water alive and abundant at the Vigil have responded to this challenge in several ways. (See the article, "Fonts for Function and Meaning," by S. Anita Stauffer in *Catechumenate: A Journal of Christian Initiation,* March, 1988, 22–29.) For more temporary solutions, some parishes have constructed portable immersion fonts by the clever and tasteful use of wood and fiberglass or plastic pool linings. Other parishes have rented hot tubs, disguised with plants and flowers so that the values represented by such a vessel do not cloud the symbol of death and rising into Christ that is both tomb and womb, not leisure for those with means. Even with plants and flowers, it is hard to disguise a hot tub.

When infusion is the method for baptism, another common practice at the Vigil is the use of a small wading pool, decorated appropriately and placed in such a way as to harmonize with the entire environment of the liturgy. The candidate kneels in the pool and water is poured three times from a pitcher. This form of infusion speaks more loudly than the "little-dab'll-do-ya" technique and is easily accomplished with little effort and little cost. These suggestions should in no way substitute for full and permanent baptismal facilities. These interim measures can be seen as a parish gradually appropriates the fullness of symbolic expression and becomes accustomed to new avenues of expression.

Following the water bath the ritual gives no instruction about drying the candidates or about the change of clothing that will be necessary. (In the case of immersion or in the expanded form of infusion described above the candidates enter the water in bathing accouterments or some sort of appropriate clothing.) Parishes need to make arrangements for this change of clothing and for what will happen in the ritual while the changing occurs. An order of service may be this:

- The water bath.
- The presentation of the white garment. A sample pattern for the white garment can be found in the appendix of Gabe Huck's book, *The Three Days* (Chicago: Liturgy Training Publications, 1981).
- The change of clothing in another place with women's and men's facilities separate; perhaps the sacristies. Godparents assist.
- The profession of faith by the candidates for full communion, or, in their absence, the renewal of baptismal promises by the assembly and the sprinkling rite may then take place. In lieu of these two options the assembly may sing an Easter hymn.

When the neophytes return, they are welcomed with a rousing applause or a great round of "Alleluia." They are then presented with a lighted candle (#230). These candles can be specially decorated for the neophytes by the godparents or by artists in the parish. The godparent lights the candle from the Easter candle and presents it to the neophyte as the presider invites the newly baptized to "keep the flame of faith alive."

The rite calls the clothing in the white garment and the lighting of the candle "explanatory rites" (#229). Thus entitled, these two rites are images that begin to unpack the meaning of the water bath: We are clothed in Christ, finding our new identity in the Risen One, and together with Christ we are the light of the world.

Next follows the celebration of confirmation. Confirmation is an integral part of the initiatory rites of the Vigil, and any presbyter who baptizes an adult has no need to obtain permission to celebrate it. The presider first invites the community to pray for the pouring out of the Holy Spirit (#233). After a time of silence, the presider extends hands over the neophytes and says the prayer of confirmation[2] (#234). As in the rite of confirmation celebrated by a bishop, there is no formal imposition of hands at this juncture.[3] The neophytes are anointed with chrism as the presider says the words: "Be sealed with the gift of the Holy Spirit." Note that the anointing after baptism (#228) is to be omitted when confirmation is celebrated.

If the renewal of baptismal promises has not been transposed as suggested above, it occurs after the confirmation of the neophytes and before the neophytes take their places among the faithful (#237). When the sprinkling rite is completed, the newly baptized are brought to their places in the assembly and are invited to complete their initiation by sharing in two activities, both for the first time: the general intercessions and the procession to the altar with gifts (#241). The task of the baptized is to transform the world in prayer and in action that flow from and are nourished by communion with God in the Spirit.

The neophytes are given special mention during the eucharistic prayer with the proper inserts that can be found in the sacramentary in the ritual masses for Christian initiation. Peter Scagnelli translated

---

[2] For an interesting and challenging work on the history and meaning of confirmation within the baptismal synaxis, see: Aidan Kavanagh, *Confirmation: Origins and Reform* (New York: Pueblo, 1988).

[3] For a discussion of the laying on of hands in the celebration of confirmation see: Gerard Austin, *Anointing with the Spirit: The Rite of Confirmation* (New York: Pueblo, 1985), 43–45.

several inserts for this purpose from the Italian sacramentary (see *Sourcebook for Sundays and Seasons* cited previously). The inserts he translates from the Italian are much more complete in their imagery than the present ones in the English sacramentary.

Coda

The Vigil of the Paschal Memory continues to generate excitement in many parishes. Let it begin in the night, and let the celebration continue even into the Eighth Day of Easter. Let liturgists and catechists collaborate in the preparation of the event. Know the rites. Know the liturgical space. Know the assembly, its gifts and needs. Know common sense, good taste and a sense of beauty. Let the celebration begin! Join the dance and find pleasure in the fullness of springtime.

10

Blessing
of the
Baptismal Water

David N. Power

The night on which the church keeps vigil in memory of Jesus Christ's death and resurrection is a night of re-creation and rebirth. The church proclaims and celebrates the new life that is shaped by Christ's victory over sin and death and by the hope of resurrection in the Risen One. The baptismal water is the element in which God's people are reborn and become partakers in the living reality of Christ's body and the Spirit's temple, that people who are the historical presence in the world of God's saving promise and power.

In the course of the Vigil service, which is both memorial and expectation, the blessing of the waters completes the scriptural proclamation and derives its own evocative power from its integration of scriptural imagery and type. In the revision of the rites of baptism and of the Paschal Vigil that took place after the Second Vatican Council, it was felt that the standing rite of blessing in the Roman liturgy was, despite its magnificence, unsatisfactory.[1] It was written in a form that some found did not fit easily into the best traditions of liturgical blessing. While it began with thanksgiving to God the Father in a

---

[1] Cf. E. Lengeling, "Blessing of Baptismal Water in the Roman Rite," *Concilium* 22 (2/1967): 62–68.

David N. Power, OMI, is currently professor of systematic theology and liturgy in the department of theology at The Catholic University of America, Washington DC.

section that recalled the divine action in creation and history, it then took the forms of an exorcism of the water and of a direct address to the water, in which Christ's saving deeds were recalled, and finally it took the form of a petition for the descent of the Holy Spirit. It also incorporated many priestly actions such as the movement of the water with the hands, the blowing of breath upon it, the dipping of the paschal candle into the font and the mixing of oil with the water.

While it may be felt that some of the rich symbolism of this blessing was too readily discarded,[2] the need for a less-hybrid composition can be acknowledged. When we see what the composers of the new blessing did not like in the old, we understand the shape and content they wished to give to the new.

First, they wanted to maintain what was seen as the traditional structure of blessing. This combines an act of thanksgiving to God for creative and salvific action with a prayer for the sanctification of the element to be used, couched preferably in the form of an epiclesis or prayer for the coming of the Spirit. It makes clear the sacramental quality of elements blessed, that is, their relation to the sanctification of the persons who take part in the ritual of their use.

Second, they eliminated the exorcism of the waters or that prayer that was intended to drive evil spirits out of them. It did not seem proper to include such a factor in a prayer of proclamatory thanksgiving. It seemed problematic to suggest that material things are, in the order of sin, inhabited by evil spirits, at least if the words of exorcism are given literal meaning.

Third, they removed the confusion of mixing oil into the water, thus making it possible for the two rites of baptismal immersion and of anointing to retain their distinctive place in the total symbolism of the night's liturgy. They also abolished the various actions of the celebrant, though in the order approved for the United States the immersion of the candle in the pool toward the conclusion, or in conjunction with the invitation of the Spirit, is kept. This timidity with regard to gestural action in blessing may in fact be one of the losses of the new rite. It plays down the impact of the visual.

Fourth, this new composition gives greater coherence to the scriptural typologies or images used in the prayer, making clearer how the

---

[2] Cf. A. Stock, "The Blessing of the Font in the Roman Liturgy," *Concilium* 178 (2/1985): 43–52.

use of water in baptism gives neophytes a participation in the divine mysteries of creation and salvation.

Imagery

This last point is a helpful one on which to pick up in order to get further into the heart of the blessing. The old Roman prayer attached five paradigms to the action of the Father and five to the action of Christ, but strangely it omitted any recollection of the crossing of the Red Sea by the Israelite people in their escape from the slavery of Egypt. The new blessing uses two sets of triple paradigms or types, from Old and New Testament respectively. In the first set, thanks is given for the presence of the Spirit over the waters of creation, for the waters of the flood in which both the destruction of evil and the beginning of a renewed covenant with humanity were effected, and for the leading of the Israelite people across the Red Sea. In the second set it is Christ's baptism in the Jordan, the water and blood flowing from his side upon the cross and the baptismal command of Matthew 28:19 that are recalled.

It is quite clear that Christian tradition has taken all of these images as symbols or types of baptism and its saving power, or of God's saving action in baptism. They give to the prayer a rich and multicolored imagery and insert the baptismal act into the flow of history. The same creative and saving power that was operative in the first creation, in the covenant made with Noah and in the liberation of the Israelite people is operative in the rebirth through water of those who are God's people in Christ. The complexity of the biblical narratives shows that it is impossible to reduce our understanding of what is done in baptism to any single image. The relation of God to those who are called and the life of grace bestowed enrich our humanity in many ways and give us a role in human history that can be appreciated in its fullness through an appropriation of these stories and images. The creative presence of God's Spirit in the world is restored to us through baptism in Christ, and we are again enabled to find ways to live in perfect harmony with all creatures and earthly elements. The story of the flood depicts the destructive power of human evil, but still more strongly it evokes the merciful power of God which saves and delivers from evil in both personal and systemic forms. It also offers images of covenant and peace whereby to envisage the grace of baptism. Quite often in catechesis the crossing of the Red Sea has been allowed to stand for baptism through the imagery of *passing over*. In this way it contrasts two ways of life and offers an image of total conversion, which is a participation in the passage of Christ from this life to the right hand of God and the glory of the resurrection. However, even while retaining this imagery, it should be remembered that the crossing of the waters was made under God's leadership and that it was an act of liberation from slavery and destruction.

Remembrance

The anamnesis or remembrance of three significant moments in the mystery of Christ is also very powerful. Going down into the pool, his candidates descend as Christ descended into the waters of the Jordan. With him they are proclaimed as God's children, and with him they are anointed by the Holy Spirit, empowered to testify to God's life in their new lives. The cleansing action of the water that takes away sin is at the same time an act of empowerment in the Spirit, endowing candidates with new life. It is a new act of creation and rebirth. Water and blood flowing from the side of Christ are covenantal signs. They testify to the completeness of Christ's love and self-gift, to the abandon of God's mercy and to the birth of the church through baptism and eucharist. The baptismal command is that of the risen Christ who sends the disciples to take the power of his saving acts and the knowledge of God's name to the ends of the earth as a church that witnesses to Christ's authority and to salvation.

The deeds of God in both testaments are remembered in a setting of thanksgiving, which is the proper form for Christian blessing. Not only is the memory alive in the minds of those who pray, but it is alive in their hearts. The deeds of God are transformative and active in their divine energy. Their being remembered brings renewal to the spirit and calls for joy and gratitude.

Though the story and the images are powerful, it has to be admitted that the new blessing prayer is rather wooden in the way it incorporates them. A strong catechetical or instructional concern seems to have had an influence. Instead of letting the images speak in context, the prayer tells what they are supposed to signify. Toward the beginning it informs that water has been given as a rich symbol of the grace of the sacrament. It cannot refrain further on from saying in as many words that the waters of the flood and of the Red Sea are signs of baptism. It is not necessary to use that kind of vocabulary in a setting that sufficiently establishes the poetic and symbolic power of these memories and images.

Epiclesis

From the joy and gratitude of remembrance, the prayer turns to petition—a petition for the Spirit that brings God's action into the immediate assembly and to the water around which it is gathered. The composers appear to have labored somewhat over the writing of this section of the prayer, for it bears the signs of labor.

In traditional euchology, it is sometimes asked of God that the Spirit be sent and sometimes that the Spirit descend. The epiclesis of this prayer is divided into two. In the first part the request is made that the water receive the grace of the Only-begotten from the Spirit, which the English version translates "by the power of the spirit." In the second section, it is asked that the Spirit descend into the font.

The descent of the Spirit into the font makes us mindful both of creation and of the baptism of Jesus in the Jordan, and this is indicative of the power that the water has to sanctify those who descend into it. The prayer at this juncture, however, seems to have been divided into a kind of double epiclesis in order to accommodate different images of the grace of baptism.[3]

One of these images is rooted in John 3:5, where Jesus speaks to Nicodemus of rebirth through water and the Holy Spirit. This is the image used in the first part of the epiclesis, which represents the font not only as a pool of cleansing but more forcefully as a place of rebirth, or as a womb in which the candidates are newly conceived and from which they come forth to a new life.

The second traditional image comes from Romans 6:3-4, "Do you not know that all of us who have been baptized into Christ Jesus were baptized into his death? We were buried therefore with him by baptism into death, so as Christ was raised from the dead by the glory of the Father, we too might walk in newness of life." This

---

[3] Cf. G. Winkler, "The Blessing of Water in the Oriental Liturgies," ibid., 53-61.

burial and resurrection with Christ through the water of baptism is made the object in the prayer of blessing of the second petition for the Holy Spirit's action.

As far as Paul was concerned, death with Christ brought with it death to sin or even victory over sin, which is a more powerful image. Together with release from sin, it brought release from death, to be assured most certainly in the resurrection of the flesh but already given in some measure to the baptized. In ascetical writings or even in catechesis, the image of death and resurrection in Christ often has been used to emphasize the reality of death to sin or to encourage a desire for conversion. Paul's vision of baptism into the death that signals Christ's victory over sin and death connotes the beginning of a life that is to be crowned by the resurrection of the flesh in Christ's victory over God's enemies. If this is kept in mind, the images of rebirth and of baptism into Christ's death exist together in a creative and suggestive tension. The Holy Spirit works within the water and in those baptized to bring them into communion with Christ's victory through his death over sin and death itself and enlivens in them the hope of the resurrection.

The text approved for use in the United States allows for the lowering of the Easter candle into the font between the two parts of the petition. This conjoins the image of the Pasch of Christ with the action of the Spirit in the water. The Pasch of Christ is the deed through which the creative power of the Spirit is newly released, as it is the mystery into whose communion the grace of the Spirit introduces the baptized.

Actions

This is a welcome but somewhat minimal retrieval of the presider's gestures over the water. It may be conceded that mixing oil with the water or blowing breath over the pool is not appropriate. Some movement of the water, however, is desirable, lest the water become only secondary to the imagery of death and new life instead of a constitutive part of it. How the font is constructed, how much water it contains, whether it permits the candidates to get into it, are matters of prime importance for the power of the blessing to relate to the power of the baptismal action. That the people see the water and that their attention be drawn to it from the very beginning of the blessing is very important, for otherwise the images of water are not present to the mind in the recollection of the biblical types and in the prayer for the action of the Spirit. In that case, types and prayer would lose much of their force.

The symbolism of baptism that is brought to the fore in the prayer does after all begin with the water itself, and water of its very nature evokes images of life and death. The traditional catechesis of baptism is replete with the eulogies of water. In the words of Tertullian, it is a "material always perfect, cheerful, simple and naturally pure." Having praised it in many ways, he concludes:

> If I were to go on and recount all or even most of what could be said about the importance of this element—the greatness of its power or value, the number of its qualities, of its functions, and of its uses in the world—I fear I would appear to have composed a panegyric on water rather than an explanation of baptism; though were I to do so, it would serve to show more fully that there is no ground for doubting that God has brought into service in his own sacraments the same material element that he has employed in all his acts and dealings and that the material that directs our earthly life makes provision for our heavenly life as well.[4]

Some stirring of the water by the hand of the presider at the beginning of the blessing could stimulate the imagination of all present, causing them to have before them the qualities, functions and uses of the water. The images of creation and redemption that the prayer evokes would then ring all the more powerfully in their ears.

Congregation

A further note on the images of rebirth and new life in the blessing of the water has to do with their relation to the congregation into which the candidates are to be baptized. Nowadays, both the blessing and the baptism are done in full view of the assembly. The expediency of this is arguable, but at least it serves to remind us that the candidates are to become a living part of a community and that the power of the water in the Spirit is no more or less than the power of the

---

[4] Tertullian, *On Baptism,* excerpted in M. Wiles and M. Santer (eds.), *Documents in Early Christian Thought* (Cambridge: Cambridge University Press, 1979), 175.

Spirit in the parental community of the faithful. If the water is to serve as a womb of re-creation and rebirth, this is within a community that is itself a living organism within which new life is fashioned and of which the baptized become, throughout the stages of the catechumenate, a vital part. If the water is to give a share in the victory of Christ's death over sin and forces of destruction, the living embodiment of that power must be already evident in the Christian congregation. If the pool is to contain the promise of the resurrection, the candidates must already have received testimony of that promise from the words and deeds of the community that welcomes them. The community of the faithful, with its own history and specific qualities and gifts, is always the context within which sacramental prayer and action take place and from which they take their meaning and power. If Christ and the Spirit are not alive in the community, we cannot realistically evoke their life-giving presence in the water. Fulfilling the mandate of Christ to baptize is done by those who have accepted the invitation to believe and to become followers.

Conclusion

Many things then, serve to bring the meaning of the rite of water blessing to life. First, there is the community of the faithful that has welcomed the candidates and accompanied them with its witness and its ministry. Second, there are the candidates who have learned to believe and who, like the hart, yearn for running streams. Third, there is the water, creature of simplicity and of magnificence, apt reflection of all the earth's forces of destruction, of life, of cleansing and of refreshment. Fourth, there are the biblical stories and types, vibrant in the memory of their telling through the lenten season and on this night of vigil. Fifth, there is the lighted candle of Easter, symbol of this night of nights on which the church keeps vigil, glowing reminder of a night turned into day, of darkness overcome by light, of death overpowered by the death of God's Son, of a life given, never to be extinguished. Sixth and finally, there is the movement of the Spirit over the waters, its descent into the pool, at once tomb and womb, creating the world anew in the image of Christ and in the love of God.

11

Renunciation of
Evil and Profession
of Faith

Robert W. Hovda

In the years since 1972 and the promulgation of the RCIA, I have come across no more honest and insightful summary of its significance than this paragraph from a paper by Ralph Keifer in 1974:

> The attempt to reform the rites of initiation has issued in the promulgation of rites that are, historically and culturally speaking, a massive rejection of the presuppositions both of pastoral practice and of most churchgoers regarding the true meaning of church membership. This is a revolution quite without precedent, because the Catholic church has never at any time in its history done such violence to its ritual practice as to make its rites so wholly incongruous with its concrete reality. Such an act is either a statement that rite is wholly irrelevant, or a statement that the church is willing to change, and to change radically, that concrete reality. Such an approach is either suicide or prophecy of a very high order.[1]

What was a whisper in the first teaching document of the Second Vatican Council became a mighty roar with RCIA: the recovery from

---

[1] "Christian Initiation: The State of the Question," *Made, Not Born*, (Murphy Center for Liturgical Research, University of Notre Dame Press, 1976): 149–50.

Robert W. Hovda, priest of the diocese of Fargo, writes "The Amen Corner" as a regular feature of *Worship* and lectures frequently on issues of ecclesial and liturgical renewal.

centuries of neglect, the rediscovery of local church—church on the concrete level of the baptized community of faith, the assembly that gathers on Sunday. But most of us were not (and are not today) prepared to undertake the pastoral work presupposed and demanded by liturgical reform in general and by initiation in particular: ensuring "that the faithful take part fully aware of what they are doing, actively engaged in the rite and enriched by its effects" *(Constitution on the Sacred Liturgy, #11)*.

Even apart from the obvious current reaction against the conversion and labor of reform, we do not yet seem to understand that the project is not a substitution of new texts or new gestures or new furnishings for old, but rather a penetration of all these to their foundation, their author, the Sunday assembly, the church and the virtual rediscovery of that local, concrete community of faith. So the ritual books no longer "give us the liturgy," detailed and complete. They give us only the tradition, the structure, and it is the living assembly who, by being "actively engaged in the rite," makes a liturgy of it.

Leaders and planners, therefore, are responsible to the assembly or church as well as to the books and the tradition. "More is required than the mere observance of the laws governing valid and lawful celebration" (CSL, #11). It is a job description for clergy and other leaders that is new to many. I make these prefatory remarks, risking repetition, because the following comments are tentative and untried, and it is only testing and experience in the flow of the rite that will prove whether they enhance meaning in a particular time and place and thereby promote the active engagement of all. Much careful and measured experiment will have to precede satisfactory solutions.

My job here is to look at the profession of faith and its renewal in the Easter Vigil's initiation sacraments and suggest possible ways of doing them that might be more engaging and that might avoid some of the problems of the present arrangement. My suggestions are organized in relation to these three problems: 1. The problem of duplication, with "separate but equal" promises, first, for the elect before their baptisms, and later, for those received into full communion and the rest of the assembly. 2. The problem of language, including both questions about the appropriateness of terms and an excessive reliance on verbal formulae. 3. The problem of clericalism and the proper role of the presider.

The Problem of Duplication

There is no doubt a difference between making these promises for the first time and to the community into which one is being initiated (the situation of the elect) and the renewal of promises already made (the situation of the rest of the assembly). But that difference can be exaggerated, for baptism does not end the struggle in our lives between God and idolatry. Christian life is a pattern of struggle, of paschal dying, letting go and being raised up in new life, over and over again. Christian initiation brings the struggling one into a company where strength for the battle is available in the sharing of the Spirit, the tradition and mutual support.

It seems to me that we can respect the difference and still avoid the duplication if the candidates for baptism are at this point standing facing the rest of the assembly and are invited by the presider separately and first to renounce idols and to worship God. Then the presider can turn to the rest of the assembly and invite renewal. It is the faith of the church we are confessing, not a mere private or individual insight. So it would seem appropriate that the whole church would support and join in this avowal, using its classic credal form, with the elect facing and leading the rest. All except the elect would be holding lighted candles again as from the kindling of the light through the Easter proclamation.

Such a solution would permit the sprinkling of the assembly to occur immediately after the baptisms of the neophytes. After immersion, neophytes leave the assembly for a few minutes to discard wet garments, dry themselves and don basic fresh clothing over which a baptismal garment will be placed when they return to the assembly. Immersion is clearly preferable and must become the practical norm, either in fonts (small pools) built for the purpose or by pouring water over the entire body while the person stands or kneels in a temporary pool too shallow to receive the whole being.

If there is any feeling in the community that this solution deprives it of the opportunity to hear directly from the elect, the latter could be invited to make very brief (100 words or less) statements before the common profession of faith. I don't think this would be necessary, but it is certainly possible. It would indicate why he or she desires to be part of Christ's church and would be carefully formulated as part of one's preparation for the event.

It is important here to discuss the manner and extent of sprinkling, both in the Easter Vigil and regularly on Sundays. In a large assembly, a single minister traversing the aisles rapidly cannot do it appropriately. It takes time to make sure that each row is included and every last person in the assembly feels the water. It also takes strong, firm aspergilla and pitching arms. The branches of trees and plants look lovely, but few are strong enough to propel the water drops to the farthest reaches of each row. Several ministers, each with an aspergillum and a bucket, may be required—each responsible for a part of the assembly and with the time to do it right.

The Problem of Language

Suggestions here regarding texts and language are based on a few general principles. Communications experts assure us that body language, environment, attitudes conveyed by one's mien and other nonverbals are more powerful messengers than our words and "content." But, while that power is strong, it is also subtle. So it is easier for people to blame reformed rites for their disappointment when they should be blaming our failure to provide adult education, appropriate environments and ministerial training for the effective use of the rites.

Another principle is the difference between God's word and our efforts to interpret it in terms of our mission and action in daily life. Revelation commands only that our mission be liberating and reconciling for all humanity in the holy One and that the means be conformable to love. The means themselves, our concrete steps, action, legislation, etc., our inching the world along—these are our responsibility, subject to human error, and it is out of a great variety of interpretations that the church prays for a consensus to emerge and a living tradition to grow. The liturgy, where scripture and sacrament constitute our primary and indispensable sources, prefers and insists on a classic, universal, seminal, symbolic articulation of Christian mission or moral imperative, in contrast to a party line of specific and concrete applications.

The biblical covenant is also clear on the principle that the basic sin and the ground of all sin is idolatry, so any renunciation of evil in the moral sense is a renouncing, a rejection, a deflating of our idols. On the basis of these principles, then, the current lack among most believers of a strong sense of this liberating and reconciling mission or moral imperative suggests that it has not been a part of our formation and that it must be stressed (in compensation for neglect) in adult education, preaching, intercessions, all the way through the catechumenate and articulated forcefully at this moment. Whether the personification of evil in Satan (renunciation questions) is a sufficiently vivid and strong figure today is a question. Nor do "sin" and "the glamor of evil" have the force we need—because moral issues have shrunk for so many to the tiny dimensions of sex.

While it would involve exceptional talents and a lot of work to do it beautifully and appropriately, perhaps nonverbals could come to our aid at the point of renunciation. Some kind of visual representation of our major contemporary idols—e.g., money, property, coercive power, "dog eat dog" competition, "putting down" sex, color, class, social status groups different from one's own—might be used effectively. A picture is worth a thousand words. If those idols were simply and boldly represented and easily recognizable from the farthest point in the assembly, they could advance on each of the elect and be dispelled by the candidate's holding up the cross. Experimentation with efforts at such representation (in brief dramatic forms, in posters or placards or projected slides, in mime) would soon reveal possibilities and problems.

If we stay with verbal affirmation, I recommend the additions, following the creed, in the Episcopal church's proposed *Book of Common Prayer.*[2] Four additional questions in this book make a bit more explicit what may be too subtle in the previous symbolic language, although even these questions could be more pungent without overstepping the bounds of revelation.

Although the renouncing part of the avowals needs attention, I would be satisfied with the profession of the church's faith in the saying or singing of the Apostles' Creed. It would probably be strong if a historic creed were not part of every Sunday's liturgy. It hardly seems necessary in a liturgy that is a profession of faith from beginning to end to insert the creed and thereby interrupt the flow from gospel to homily to intercessions. At any rate, that classic statement, with its origins in baptismal practice, has not yet been improved upon for this moment of common affirmation of a common faith.

[2] The Church Hymnal Corporation and the Seabury Press, 1988, 293–94.

The Problem of Clericalism

The way in which the texts (questions and answers) are handled in the rite can be improved dramatically to correspond to our recovery of an ecclesiology of the local church, by a reversal of the roles indicated in the current rites. *The Book of Common Prayer*, mentioned above, has perceived this and has the presider asking only enough to elicit the assembly's proclamation of each of the three parts of the creed. Our rite, unfortunately, has the presider proclaiming the creed and the assembly reduced to two-syllable replies. Such replies are much too weak to bear the weight of this moment of intense ecclesial consciousness. We are church, all of us who are baptized and part of the assembly, and we should act like church, not like patients or clients or consumers or passive recipients.

If we have made initiation and the involvement of the entire faith community in the initiation process the top priority in our local church, our Sunday assembly, then we are on the right track. And we can take our time in testing ways of educing the meaning, the vital dynamic of the rite's words and actions—ways suggested by a lively liturgical imagination. Better ways will come out of serious experimentation...and the sharing of its results.